Dear Reader:

AMI Books is proud to bring you an exciting new series straight from the files of the National Enquirer, America's favorite tabloid. Now, every month, we will be going in-depth to bring you the whole story.

The book you are about to read is based on the work of some of the top award-winning investigative journalists in the world. If you're looking for the inside scoop on topics ranging from the most sensational crimes captivating our nation to Hollywood profiles that show the tragedy under the tinsel, you'll find it here.

For over thirty years, *The National Enquirer* has been telling it like it is to more than thirteen million readers a week — and now we're going to take you deep into the Enquirer's confidential files to bring you the untold stories behind the headlines.

Valerie Virga
President, AMI Books

From the files of
The National Enquirer

SEX, POWER
& MURDER

Chandra Levy
and Gary Condit
— the affair that
shocked America

By DAVID WRIGHT and DON GENTILE
with NICHOLAS MAIER

American Media Inc.

FROM THE FILES OF THE NATIONAL ENQUIRER:
SEX, POWER & MURDER

Copyright © 2002 AMI Books, Inc.

Cover design: Martin Elfers
Cover photograph of Chandra Levy: Zuma Press;
Gary Condit: AP/Wideworld Photo

ISBN: 1-885840-01-2

First printing: October, 2002

Printed in the United States of America

10 9 8 7 6 5 4 3 2 1

PROLOGUE

Tuesday, May 1, 2001, dawned bright and beautiful in Washington, D.C., with temperatures headed for a high of 82. The strong sun rose in a clear blue sky, the blooming magnolias scented the air, and around the chalk white buildings of the nation's capital, the landscape was alive with fresh color.

For such a glorious start, this day would come to a tragic end.

Chandra Levy, after closing her blinds to block out the light, sat down at a space-saver desk built into a closet in her small apartment. Her long, curly black hair flowed down below petite shoulders, and her warm hazel eyes fell to the screen of a laptop computer. She was soon clicking her way through four media Web sites that featured articles about George W. Bush's luncheon the day before, all of them noting that Congressman Gary Condit held a place of honor at the President's table.

Chandra, an energetic and promising woman from California, had everything in the world to look forward to. She was only twenty-four, with an endearing smile. Intelligent and confident, she'd gotten a master's degree in public administration from the University of Southern California, and was set to attend her graduation ceremony in just a few days. She was fit and healthy, with a life of desires and hopes yet to be realized.

Most of all, the young and attractive intern was engaged in a tempestuous sexual affair and falling deeply in love with a powerful congressman some thirty years her senior.

Totally absorbed, Chandra read and reread the dispatch of Marc Sandalow, the Washington bureau chief of the San Francisco Chronicle. In it Condit was quoted as saying, "Any time you get an opportunity to break bread with the President of the United States, you should avail yourself to that opportunity."

Chandra gazed raptly at the words, dreaming of accompanying her lover to such political functions. She had tried to call him repeatedly over the last few days, desperate to hear his voice and possibly steal away for another passionate encounter. Unfortunately, that "other woman," his wife, Carolyn, was in town.

Assured by the smooth-talking congressman that she would one day be the new Mrs. Gary Condit, Chandra believed that the steamy and secretive sexual rendezvous with her man would eventually lead to a white picket fence and children running in the yard. Condit had promised as much, and she naively believed him.

The young woman's overwhelming desire to do whatever it took to please Condit led her to the next Web site.

"Chandra downloaded dozens of pictures showing breasts of different sizes," revealed a D.C. police insider. "The police didn't know what it meant, but investigators later found out that Condit is a breast man. Some investigators think Chandra thought her breasts weren't nice enough for him and that maybe she was contemplating surgery to make him happy."

In piecing together the day she vanished, authorities theorize that at one point Chandra could have agreed to meet an acquaintance at the Klingle Mansion, the three-story gray stone farmhouse built in 1823 that sat in an isolated section of Washington's Rock Creek Park, more than 1700 acres of dense woods and winding trails. The mansion contained offices and storage space for park equipment and was located a little more than two miles from Chandra's apartment and also a convenient mile from Condit's "bachelor pad" condo.

Chandra was always ultra-cautious, according to those who knew her best, and would never have ventured into the park unless she felt secure.

Still surfing the net, she went to a site called MapQuest, honing in on directions that showed the mansion's specific location. It would be easy to get there, she learned, and the warm temperature made it a great day for a stroll. She could head north from her apartment onto Connecticut Avenue, a main Washington thoroughfare, and do some window-shopping as she went.

Next, Chandra visited a site for the Baskin-Robbins ice cream chain, which has a feature that allows visitors to find the nearest shop. As luck would have it, there was a store at 2804 Connecticut Avenue NW, only thirty feet from a walkway that descended into the park.

Washington police later recalled how Chandra told her aunt Linda Zamsky that she and Condit loved to share ice cream during their time together. Linda even recalled the flavor — chocolate-chip-cookie-dough.

Chandra logged off her computer nearly four hours after sitting down and, at some point, headed out of the apartment wearing a pair of black stretch leggings, a USC T-shirt, and a pair of white Reebok tennis shoes. She was in such a rush that after washing and drying a comforter, she tossed it just inside her apartment door. Whoever she wanted to meet took priority over everything else.

Soon Chandra was in the shadows of the Klingle Mansion, the warm afternoon wearing on. There were no sounds except for the birds and the light wind in the trees.

The dense woods masked the noise of the bustling city. Chandra carried no identification, as was his rule whenever she went out with Condit — nothing but her keys, a Sony Walkman, and a small container of Baskin-Robbins ice cream. Her thoughts were filled with vivid fantasies of a happy future.

No one would ever see Chandra Levy alive again.

CHAPTER 1

Chandra Levy was born in Cleveland, Ohio, on April 14, 1977. Her mother, Susan, had an interest in Buddhism and chose the name Chandra because in Sanskrit it means "daughter higher than the moon and stars."

Warmer weather called the Levys west, and the family moved to Modesto, California, when Chandra was three. Four years later her brother, Adam, was born. The two children grew up in a privileged world with their mother sculpting in a studio in the house and their father, a successful doctor, settling into a busy medical practice. Bob Levy, a former U.S. Army lieutenant whose round face and heavy eyes are framed by a receding hairline, had earned a reputation as a doctor who never gave up on his patients.

"Last Chance Bob," his colleagues called him.

Ninety miles east of San Francisco, Modesto was, in many ways, an idyllic place to grow up, its clean streets scented by almond blossoms fed by a strong sun and the surrounding countryside dotted with strawberry fields and horse farms. It is the kind of town where neighbors always say hello and stop to discuss the weather. The town had provided the setting for the classic movie *American Graffiti*, and the sign on the main road proudly proclaimed its slogan: "Water, Wealth, Contentment, Health."

As a child, said her grandmother, Lee Pollack, Chandra looked like Betty Boop, the old-time cartoon character. She had the same pouty lips and rosy cheeks, missing only the curl in the middle of her forehead.

But this Betty Boop, unlike the ditzy cartoon character, was determined to break through stereotypes with a strong will and fierce determination. She played Little League baseball with the boys and later joined a tough summer wilderness program in which she was the only girl.

"They all asked her, 'What are you doing here?'" Susan Levy recalled, her face a mirror image of her daughter's, lighting up with the memory.

After completing the Outward Bound type course, Chandra returned to Modesto suntanned and fit. She had scaled walls, climbed ropes, and camped without any of the comforts of home. Her parents found out later that five boys had not been able to take the rigors of the class and had dropped out.

"She learned a lot about herself that summer," said Susan.

In 1995, while Chandra was a senior in high school, her family took a vacation to Ecuador, Peru, and the Galapagos Islands. Chandra demonstrated a thrill-seeker mentality that would prove telling, writing in a journal about how their guides persuaded her to swim in a lake infested with caymans, anaconda snakes, and piranhas.

"The feeling of danger and not knowing what was going to bite at any time was an adrenaline rush," Chandra wrote.

"She was so independent and confident," pointed out Susan, "that she wasn't scared of anything."

Throughout her years at Grace M. Davis High School, Chandra did well academically and earned good grades. She was popular, but also not afraid to put friendships on the line by joining the Modesto Police Department's Explorer Scout group.

The Explorers spent most of their time tracking down the owners of stray dogs or picking up trash, but Chandra was not interested in the easy tasks. Instead, she volunteered to go undercover, working with cops to bust shopkeepers who sold alcohol to underage kids. She posed as a fresh-faced buyer with no ID, and more than a few shopkeepers lived to regret seeing the attractive young woman. Chandra even went so far as to wear her Explorer uniform and badge to school.

"That really took a lot of self-confidence," marveled her history teacher, Ed Arnold. "Chandra was her own person, even as a high school student."

Chandra also surprised the friends whom she usually joined at McDonald's and Burger King by announcing one day that she was swearing off all meat, poultry, and fish, declaring herself a vegetarian.

At home there was no shortage of money, but Chandra worked to buy her first car, and after-school jobs would eventually help pay for college.

Chandra's relations with boys her own age never developed into anything more than friendship, and she went through the high school dating process with little interest. She was an admitted "daddy's girl," claiming as much time as his busy schedule allowed.

Don Vance, a lifelong friend of the Levy family, recalled the joy that Bob Levy felt participating in a parent-child summer theater production held by the local Y.M.C.A. when Chandra was a little girl.

"It was called Y Indian Princesses," said Vance. "My daughter was in it, too. We all wore vests and necklaces like Indians. We went camping and at the end of the summer had a graduation ceremony by a river at night. We took Indian names. Bob was Big Chief, and Chandra was Little Lady Bug. Bob had the time of his life."

While her teenage girlfriends debated the qualities of the boys at school or engineered their first dates, Chandra preferred to spend time with Dad. She visited his medical office and was fascinated by the mysterious cancer cells she viewed through a microscope. Later they graduated to a telescope, and drove together for three hours to the highest point in Yosemite National Park to gaze at the stars.

Despite Chandra's dedication to her father, there were clear signs that she was highly aware of her emerging sexuality. At the age of seventeen, she dared to dream of becoming a model. Two years earlier, the high school yearbook had published a sexy photograph of her posing on a balcony against a city skyline in a tight off-the-shoulder short dress with bold flowers on it.

"I wasn't really too happy about that dress," Susan Levy admitted. "She was just fifteen or so then."

But Chandra was secretly thrilled at the attention the photograph got from her classmates, and she pestered her parents until they paid $200 to commercial photographer Jon Michael Terry to take thirty glamour shots of their headstrong daughter.

Chandra's senior quote in the Davis High 1995 yearbook was, "Always have dreams. Always make them a reality." For the time being, her dream was to become a sports writer and cover the San Francisco Giants.

Chandra left home to enroll at San Francisco State University, where she covered sports for the college paper while majoring in journalism with a minor in law enforcement. In addition to classes, she also worked for the local paper, the *Modesto Bee*, compiling baseball statistics and box scores, and then worked on live broadcasts of Giants games for a local Fox TV station.

One summer she helped operate the scoreboard at Candlestick Park for her favorite team. She attended the final game of the 1989 World Series with her father after he purchased two tickets from a scalper, shelling out a considerable sum for the occasion. Adding to the excitement, Chandra's seat had been split down the middle by the earthquake that had delayed the series start. Father and daughter commiserated with each other as the Oakland A's beat the Giants 9-6.

Possibly that painful loss contributed to a change of heart — Chandra no longer wanted a career in sports journalism. A more likely theory is that the starry-eyed young woman's enthusiasm was blunted by her fellow reporters, whom she found "hard-nosed and cynical."

Susan Levy pointed out, "There was a certain conformity and she didn't like that."

Conformity was not Chandra's style.

Her mother was silently aghast when Chandra came home from college one weekend with a rose tattoo above her left ankle.

"I didn't like it, but I didn't say much about it," said Susan. "I told her it was kind of pretty — after all, I'm an artist."

She noticed that her daughter now had three piercings on each ear. And the brown hair that her mother considered Chandra's most striking feature was now dyed jet black.

The most significant interest that Chandra developed while growing up was in politics and government. As a high school senior, she wrote an account of her adventures during her family's vacation in South America, and made a point of comparing the voting systems of the countries they visited.

"Ecuador has eighteen political parties, with 1.5 million people," she noted in an article published in the *Modesto Bee*. "Everyone is required to vote by age eighteen. If they refuse, they're fired from their job.

"In Peru, people register to vote when they're seventeen and are required to vote at eighteen. Citizens must carry identification at all times. Every time a citizen votes, the ID card is stamped. Without a card, citizens can't cash checks or get a passport. Our guide exclaimed to us, 'Without that card, I am no one.'"

This love of politics and government followed Chandra into adulthood. Within a month of arriving in Los Angeles to begin graduate school at the University of Southern California, she got herself a three-month internship in the lobbying office of the city's Republican mayor, Richard Riordan. Then, in February 2000, while still studying for her master's degree in public administration, she moved to Sacramento to intern on the legal staff of Democratic Governor Gray Davis.

The light of professional direction came on, Chandra told friends, when she toured California's notorious Folsom Prison after attending a parole hearing there on behalf of the governor's office. She was fascinated by the jobs and lives of the staff who warily watched over some of the most dangerous convicts in the country.

As soon as Chandra returned to Los Angeles she spotted a job posting by the Bureau of Prisons. They were looking for an intern in their Washington, D.C., headquarters. The salary offered was $27,000 a year.

Chandra was so excited she could not wait to apply in writing. With her experience in the offices of Mayor Riordan and Governor Davis, she could easily have sought help from either one of them, but she felt she had no time to waste. She picked up the phone and called Daniel Dunne, the Bureau of Prisons spokesman.

"She indicated that she wanted to come to D.C. to work for a federal agency and she had a particular interest in law enforcement and public affairs," Dunne recalled.

In September 2000, Chandra learned she had been given the job, and there was much to be done. She needed to arrange continuing classes at USC towards her master's degree. She would have to buy a new wardrobe. She also had to find an apartment in Washington, D.C.

Her parents, secretly hurting at the thought of their daughter moving 3,000 miles away, far from the safety of their small town, comforted themselves with the knowledge that she wouldn't be completely alone. Jennifer Baker, Chandra's hometown friend and fellow graduate student, was also going to be in Washington.

As Susan Levy watched Chandra pack for the journey, she offered some words of advice, half in jest.

"Don't you become a Monica Lewinsky."

CHAPTER 2

As confident and accomplished as Chandra Levy
was, she did have one fatal flaw — she liked older
men. By the time she was heading for the nation's
capital, she had already gone through at least two steamy
affairs, and each time the impressionable young woman
had been left heartbroken.

As a teenager, Chandra met Mark Steele, a handsome
cop in her hometown of Modesto. He was intelligent,
worldly, and earmarked for promotion. Mark never grasped
the magnitude of her determination to land her first trophy
man until it was too late. Despite her inexperience, the
young woman found ways of showing her affection. Soon
enough Steele responded.

This pretty kid was street smart beyond her years as well
as book smart, he told himself, and he was impressed by
her independence in the way she had her feet so firmly
planted in life.

They embarked on a romance that somehow never
became the talk of the gossip-ridden police department.

Possibly to make sure of this, Chandra artfully began an internship.

"It's usually a rumor mill around here," marveled police spokeswoman Gail Smith, shaking her head.

The amazing shroud of secrecy with which Chandra surrounded this first passionate relationship with a man ten years her senior would later in her life become highly significant. The determined teenager was giving early notice of her ability to keep a forbidden love secret.

The affair continued after Chandra started attending San Francisco State University, where some of her friends noted her romantic preference.

"She certainly wasn't into college boys, that's for sure," said Jakob Mosur, who shared classes with Chandra. "She was very mature for her age."

"Chandra thought guys in their young twenties were not the most stable crop out there," another California friend, Michael Vanden Bosch, agreed. "She wanted a guy who was concerned, dignified, stable, respected, headed somewhere in his field."

Chandra would drive from San Francisco back to Modesto every other weekend to be with Steele. Even so, "she wouldn't say too much about it," remarked Mosur. "Just that he was a police officer and the relationship was important to her."

But sadly, by the time the end of the affair came, it had become much too important to her. Chandra was now twenty-two, and her ego had been boosted enormously by the lengthy relationship. She had taken the bold step of introducing Steele to her parents, and was delighted when they came to accept and like him.

Chandra was convinced that she and the policeman would happily marry. Instead, Steele gently told her in August 1999 that they had to cool the relationship.

Chandra was devastated. She refused to accept the fact that she had been dumped and began bombarding the man with telephone calls, pleading with him to give their love another chance.

"Her feelings were very intense," explained a close friend.

Steele, who had been as secretive as Chandra about their romance, refused to bend, and in fact would be married to someone else within a year. At the end of the summer, Chandra reluctantly accepted the inevitable and took her broken heart to Los Angeles and graduate school at the University of Southern California.

A friend who met her then said that when she arrived on campus she was still shattered by the breakup with Steele.

"It was like she was searching for love in all the wrong places," explained the acquaintance. "She was so level-headed in most ways but seemed to have a blind spot when it came to her own relationships."

For her second love, Chandra found a man who was even older than Mark Steele, and also a doctor, like her father. Add into the mix one more adventurous sexual step for Chandra — this man was married.

Once again, she kept the relationship a closely guarded secret. It was a great romance for her, and nothing more than a brief fling for him. The affair lasted only a few months.

"The older men she's loved have grown cold and dumped her — and now she has a need to prove that it wasn't something in her that lost that man," said Dr. Joyce Brothers, the renowned psychologist. "She knows she's desirable — and she proves it by successfully going for another older or married man, and it becomes a pattern."

"She was no Virgin Mary," said psychiatrist Dr. Judianne Densen-Gerber more bluntly. "She manipulated men by her sexuality. Sex would mean very little to her except as a tool. Conquering older men made her feel powerful. She was in love with a fantasy."

Dr. Carole Lieberman, a noted Beverly Hills psychiatrist and a member of the clinical faculty at University of California at Los Angeles Neuropsychiatric Institute, added, "What women like her are acting out is missing a father figure. Fathers who are workaholics, like busy doctors, may love their daughters, but how much time can they give them throughout their childhood? By dating older men, she is looking for a true father figure to give her the full-time attention she never had."

Bearing out Dr. Lieberman's analysis, one of Bob Levy's colleagues, the anesthesiologist Mitchell Major, remembered how hard Chandra's dedicated father worked. "I'd run into him, not infrequently, taking care of patients at nine or ten at night."

"And why married men?" Lieberman continued. "That's to do with competition with her mother for whatever love and attention her father did have time to give the family. She would be jealous that her mother was getting more than she was.

"Chandra wasn't promiscuous or out for a good time. Rather she was very vulnerable and sensitive and always had a long-term relationship in mind."

Proving Lieberman correct, Chandra confided in a close friend at USC her great frustration at the now familiar story of how she had dated another man and then been dumped. According to Lisa DePaulo, a reporter who covered the story for Talk Magazine, the friend finally became exasperated and began to lecture her.

"He's been married for twenty-five years. He's twenty years older than you are. He's got kids. What did you think was going to happen? Did you really think he was going to leave his kids?"

Regardless, when the man ended the affair, it was another crushing blow.

"But that didn't register with her," said the friend. "I told her, 'Chandra, it's OK if you like older men, but older married men? Don't you think you're asking for trouble?' Chandra was such a great person. I always wondered why she was involved in these relationships that would inevitably have a bad ending."

CHAPTER 3

Gary Condit was born on April 21, 1948, in Locust Grove, Oklahoma. His father, Adrian, was a Baptist minister, and his mother, Jean, a homemaker; together they raised their three sons and one daughter on a dairy farm. As a cute, blond boy with a high tenor voice, the future lawmaker used to stand on tree stumps in the 1950s and sing *Amazing Grace* to warm up revival crowds before his dad began preaching.

Condit's grandfather and uncle were also fundamentalist preachers, and Gary and his siblings grew up in a household that banned drinking, smoking, and dancing. The kids were expected to attend church four times a week. It was the kind of strict upbringing that might eventually push a young person in the opposite direction.

And Condit soon developed a rebellious nature, acting out and getting into serious trouble with the local police. As a teen, he ignored three citations in a year — for speeding, running a stop sign, and driving without a license — before a warrant was eventually issued for his arrest. Despite the strict family ban on liquor, he was also a dedicated underage drinker with a record for skipping school.

"A James Dean kinda guy," is the way one classmate, Tulsa attorney Gary Underwood, remembered Condit. "I still have this mental image of him in high school chugging whisky with a Jack Daniel's bottle tilted up to his lips."

His wild reputation was well established by the time he met Carolyn Berry, a fellow junior at Nathan Hale High School in Tulsa.

Carolyn, in contrast, was described by a friend as "almost naive, she was so sweet."

"He changed his ways," said another acquaintance who credited Carolyn with persuading her husband to quit drinking, one habit he's never resumed. "He knew there was no way to have Carolyn other than to straighten up."

But life together for the son of a minister and the daughter of a clothing store owner began, by Bible Belt values, under a distinctly dark cloud.

Shortly after their high school graduation, Gary and Carolyn turned up at a Justice of the Peace's office in Miami, Oklahoma, and applied for a marriage license. She was only eighteen years old. Gary was also eighteen, but on the marriage application he claimed to be twenty-five. He did not dare ask his father for permission to wed.

The ceremony went ahead on January 18, 1967, on the third floor of the brown brick Ottawa County courthouse, with only a seventy-year-old worker as a witness.

It soon became apparent that Carolyn, despite her attempts, had not managed to completely straighten out her husband. Late one night a few months after the wedding, a Tulsa police officer, Rick Knight, gave chase after a brand-new, shiny bright yellow Corvette sped by him doing 65 mph on a quiet street. The automobile vanished, but

Officer Knight found it soon after parked in a driveway.

Behind the wheel sat Condit and next to him was Carolyn, who just days beforehand had given birth to the couple's first child, a boy named Chad, born on July 18th. Condit was placed under arrest for reckless driving, and the officer notified his father, already mortified by his son's marriage.

With the reassignment of Adrian Condit to a new Baptist church, the entire family, plus Carolyn and Chad, moved with him to Ceres, California. Condit welcomed the move as a chance to distance himself from Carolyn's parents, who were less than approving of their new son-in-law.

Gary soon worked his way through California State University at Stanislaus, but made little impression there.

"Condit was not a good student," said his political science teacher, John Wold. "And he was married and had a kid."

Nevertheless, in 1972 Condit found his true calling and ran successfully for his first political office — a seat on the Ceres City Council. People called him "the Boy Wonder" as his new career took off. In 1974 when he was twenty-six and only two years out of college, he became mayor of the small rural town. At thirty-five, he was making his name in the state assembly in Sacramento. At forty-one, Condit was elected to the U.S. House of Representatives.

His wife Carolyn "is a typical wife you see at the local grocery store," said Sandy Lucas, a Democratic official and friend. "She decided to keep the home fires burning while he moved up the political ladder."

Pat Paul, a county official, added, "She did what good political wives do: she smiled, she greeted people."

Carolyn's close friends in the Central Valley region talk of her passionate and endless public work on her politician husband's behalf in the 18th Congressional District.

"She was always there for him," said an admirer.

Most Wednesdays, Carolyn joined the members of a local women's club, the Soroptimists, for lunch at the Peachtree restaurant. She shared their dedication to civic projects such as the fight against teenage pregnancy and was an admirable surrogate for her busy husband stuck in Washington.

Paying a tribute to Carolyn's constituency work that is typical of what many people in the district express, Leona Garrison, an eighty-six-year-old retired Ceres city clerk, said spiritedly, "She's just a wonderful lady. She comes over and we visit a little and she takes me to have my hair done. She is just so sweet to me."

It was due in no small part to Carolyn's tireless help in the Central Valley that her husband was electorally unbeatable.

Condit campaigned under the slogan "Setting a Good Example," and he never passed up an opportunity to pick up a vote. The conservative Democrat would be returned to Washington seven times by adoring voters in northern California.

There were many examples of Condit's tireless efforts on behalf of constituents. When Debra Whitlock was murdered in Modesto, the congressman put up a reward to help catch her killer. He made a substantial contribution to find the attacker of Stanislaus County clerk-recorder Karen Mathews. He also assisted Sally Goehring in a fight against the parole application of the man convicted of murdering her cousin.

"Gary has a real good rapport with crime victims, and he's always there for them," declared Goehring.

Campaigning on a moral agenda that made his father

proud, Condit grew highly visible in Bible-study meetings held by congressional staffers and House members, and he favored legislation in 1999 to allow the Ten Commandments to be posted in school classrooms. Church was meant to be mixed with state, as he saw it.

If Congressman Condit was presented with a problem he couldn't solve immediately, he had a winning way of looking a person in the eye and saying softly, "I need to pray on it."

Every October, Condit hosted a popular community event, a picnic and fund-raiser in Ceres that was called "Condit Country." It typically drew more than 5,000 constituents eager to shake hands with the charming Democratic congressman with the confident smile who routinely won reelections by a seventy percent margin, despite the fact that the 18th District was becoming increasingly Republican.

"The voters seem to get me and understand me," Condit bragged. "The politicos have a more difficult time."

Those "politicos" grew to include members of his own party. The renegade representative had frequently earned the hostility of fellow Democrats by backing Republican initiatives in the House and refusing to back President Clinton's economic stimulus package in 1993. If Condit believed in a cause, he wasn't afraid to cross lines to support it.

He went so far as to express moral shock when the scandal of Clinton's affair with intern Monica Lewinsky blew open, urging the president to come clean and tell all, declaring piously, "Only when we strip away the cloak of secrecy and lay the facts on the table can we begin to resolve this matter honestly and openly."

CHAPTER 4

One spring day in 1972, a young Ceres City councilman, Gary Condit, and one of his colleagues strolled through San Francisco's red light district during a break in a conference meeting. The two men exchanged glances as they rounded a corner and saw several scantily dressed hookers trying to attract the attention of men in cars passing by.

"Women!" the twenty-four-year-old fledgling politician blurted out contemptuously. "As far as I'm concerned, they're here to use, abuse, and dispose of."

Those words say a lot about the secret life Condit lived even as his public life flourished and he rose through the political ranks to become a popular and powerful seven-term U.S. congressman. Although on Capitol Hill few appeared to stand straighter than Representative Gary Condit, when he escaped from Washington it was often into a seedy netherworld where he donned leather chaps and roared off on his Harley-Davidson to Hells Angels rallies around the country.

Condit ignored the titters from other House members when he posed as "Mr. June" in the 1998 "Hunks of the Hill" calendar. He later appeared nonchalantly in pictures for the raunchy biker magazine *Easyrider*. And he reveled in his Capitol Hill nickname, "Mister Blow Dry," an ironic bow to his never-a-hair-out-of-place appearance.

When safely beyond the Beltway, he thought nothing of hanging out at wet T-shirt contests. Openly gawking at the participants, he handed out his congressional card to nubile young women. It was his most effective pickup trick — one in the crowd would always call.

"In one theory of government, Condit has done a fairly good job of representing his constituents, voting their conservative values," observed Larry Sabato, a professor of government at the University of Virginia and author of *Dirty Little Secrets: The Resurgence of Corruption in American Politics*. "But he has not been a very good trustee — a person who should embody those values."

Unlike most national politicians, from the start of his long career in Washington, Gary Condit left his wife back home in Ceres. Carolyn stayed in their four-bedroom, $200,000 ranch house because, she told friends, she "wanted the kids to be established there."

Three thousand miles away, her husband bought a bachelor pad condo in the Adams Morgan neighborhood of Washington, the epicenter of the hard-partying young crowd drawn to the power and excitement of the nation's capital.

"Gary so desperately wants to stay young," said a friend.

So he was "Gary," not "Dad," to his son Chad and daughter Cadee.

"It's the Peter Pan syndrome," said Beverly Hills psychiatrist Carole Lieberman. "He can't bear the thought that he's old enough to be a daddy and have a father's responsibilities. He doesn't want to grow up — he wants to be a player forever."

Condit loved to recount how he once dove into the mosh pit to slam dance with kids at a Pearl Jam concert. He was also quick to brag about how he landed a bit part in the 1988 movie *Return of the Killer Tomatoes*. Alongside the then unknown George Clooney, Condit played a nameless "pizzeria patron." The totally forgettable movie was panned by critics, and never led to a Hollywood career for Condit.

Back in 1988, when he was a state assemblyman in Sacramento, the political magazine *California Journal* tagged Condit as "a flamboyant party boy who uses his prestige as an assemblyman to fuel a busy life."

As he rose to national recognition, Condit apparently changed little. Thirteen years later, a Washington political writer would call him "a vain, blow-dried official with a tomcat reputation."

No one knows Condit's seamy side better than Vince Flammini, a burly former weightlifter and bodybuilder who spent almost a decade as the congressman's confidante, driver, and bodyguard.

Even the most faithful voters of the Central Valley would be shocked if they saw Flammini's collection of photographs showing his boss cavorting with a group of buxom dancers in G-strings and high heels at a huge biker rally in Laughlin, Nevada, in April 1995.

"They show Gary Condit drooling over scantily clad girls young enough to be his daughter," Flammini described. "It was Gary's idea of hog heaven. He was beside himself with excitement. Whenever a girl finished her dance, he would rush up to take her hand and help her off the stage.

"I remember thinking, 'What the hell are you doing, Gary?' It's one thing to admire a pretty face, but what was a congressman, a preacher's son, and a married man with kids doing playing around with a bunch of girls barely out of their teens? The answer is he just can't help himself. He's totally obsessed with women."

According to Flammini, Condit even used his wife to gain sympathy from potential lovers. Since as far back as the sixth grade, sources say, Carolyn periodically suffered migraines. Baffled at first, she finally came to believe the headaches were the lingering result of childhood encephalitis, and in recent years they've been brought under control.

Condit would tell other women that his wife suffered from "encephalitis of the brain."

Flammini had his own theories regarding the headaches.

"In all the years I knew the two of them, I never saw Gary kiss his wife — not even so much as a peck on the cheek. He didn't even sit next to her when I drove them around in the car. Gary sat up front next to me while she sat by herself in the back. Gary listened to country and western music on the radio, and if Carolyn started to talk, he just turned up the radio to drown her out."

To make matters worse, Flammini says, Condit to this day holds a bitter grudge toward Carolyn's parents over their reaction to the forced marriage.

"I wasn't good enough for them when I married their daughter, but now that I'm a United States congressman it's a different story," Condit explained to Flammini. "Well, not to me it isn't!"

Flammini added that Mrs. Berry came to Ceres to visit and "he didn't say one word to her all the time she was there."

Nevertheless, said Flammini, Carolyn Condit still adores her husband. "She will always be loyal to him, but I think her heart is split in a million pieces.

"I asked her up front once, 'How do you put up with it?' She looked at me and said, 'Vince, I just love him so much I can't stand it. I worship the water he walks on.' To this day, I don't know if she was joking or not."

Flammini recalled a story dating back to when Condit first moved to the state capital.

The politician sipped soda water and held court in the popular Sacramento nightspot Paragary's Bar and Oven with other young lawmakers, inviting sexy college girls and secretaries over to their reserved corner table. That was when he was tagged with the nickname Hard Cock Condit.

"The nickname spread quickly," said Flammini. "As a prank, girls used to call his house. They'd say, 'Can I speak to Hard Cock Condit please?' Then they'd hang up.

"Condit explained it by saying it was the work of Republican dirty tricksters who were trying to unseat him. It was a preposterous story, but amazingly, it was enough to do the trick.

"The most amazing thing about Gary," Flammini went on, shaking his head, "Was that he never saw anything wrong in what he was doing. He'd say to me, 'God and I have an arrangement. There's nothing wrong with men having affairs. We've been doing it for thousands of years.'

"Everywhere he went he was constantly scanning around, looking for the next girl to try his silver tongue on. He'd smile, introduce himself and hand out his card. He'd pause for a few moments, waiting for the girl to read the card and be suitably impressed with the words written on it: 'Congressman Gary Condit.'

"Then, still smiling, he'd say to the star-struck girl, 'If I can ever do anything for you, give me a call.' That pickup routine worked every time. The girls were so flattered to think that this charming, handsome U.S. congressman was paying attention to them, they were eating out of his hand in no time."

Stephen Schoenthaler, professor of sociology and criminal justice at California State University at Stanislaus, explained it this way: "Some powerful married men think they have the right to pursue relationships on the side with younger women. They consider it a perk to which they're entitled, and point out that other powerful men throughout the ages have done the same thing — men such as John F. Kennedy and Franklin Roosevelt, for example."

If anyone felt entitled to sexual perks, it was the publicly buttoned-down congressman from California.

Incredibly, said Flammini, Condit would sometimes fly from Washington to San Francisco to spend weekends with another attractive young woman and then, sexually sated, fly back. Often, his family wouldn't even know he'd left Washington.

Flammini's phone would occasionally ring in the middle of the night. When he picked it up, he heard the sounds of a couple making love.

"I always believed it was Gary calling, because he loved to let me know about all the extramarital sex he was getting and it was also just the kind of thing he would think was a big joke."

Flammini said Condit freely bragged that he had been successfully cheating on his wife since they were in high school.

"He had at least four cell phones and called most of his girlfriends every day," the bodyguard charged.

"He got a kick out of being in control of a network of

women, and when he wasn't talking to them, he was bragging about them. He'd say to me, 'I have three girlfriends in Sacramento, two in Washington, another in Louisiana who keeps bugging me.' And everywhere we went, he was always on the lookout for new conquests.

"Gary kept a little yellow address book with his girlfriends listed by code names, and their phone numbers were coded, too," said Flammini. "It was a grubby, well-used little book held together with a couple of rubber bands. When I'd ask him how he could keep up with so many girlfriends, he'd just laugh and say, 'It's like hunting. There's nothing like the thrill of the chase.'

"Coffee shops, fund raisers, airplanes — Gary never missed an opportunity to pick up another girl. He was a predator, pure and simple."

CHAPTER 5

Chandra arrived in Washington, D.C., in September 2000 to a joyful reunion with Jennifer Baker, her hometown friend and classmate at the University of Southern California.

It was, the two friends exulted, the perfect time for women such as themselves — young, ambitious, and intrigued by politics — to be living in the nation's capital. Bill Clinton was in the waning months of a tumultuous presidency, Governor George W. Bush and Vice President Al Gore were crisscrossing the country battling for the right to succeed him, and the election stood only weeks away.

Chandra's parents had agreed to pick up the tab for an apartment in one of the nicer areas of Washington after their daughter said she felt unsafe across the river in Arlington, Virginia. She was always ultra cautious, and they supported that.

One visit to look at Number 315 at the Newport, a ten-story building on 21st Street NW in the upscale Dupont

Circle neighborhood, was enough for Chandra. It was safe, it was less than a dozen blocks from the White House, and Chandra instantly fell in love.

The apartment was little more than a single 500 square-foot furnished room, its walls painted white. There was a platform bed with built-in storage drawers, and a sofa and chair were pulled up to a glass-topped coffee table. A small kitchen area was separated from the living space by a waist-high counter. Picture windows, shielded by vertical blinds, looked out on the tree-lined street. Tucked in a large closet with double doors was a space-saver desk she could work on.

Another plus was that because the Newport was in the heart of the city, Chandra didn't need a car. The subway and gym were only a short walk away, and so was the exciting Georgetown area. The neighborhood streets were lined with stylish restaurants, bars, and shops.

Chandra opened her laptop computer on the desk and sent an e-mail to her parents and friends.

"I'm moved in, and I'm going to be so happy here."

The Newport, its apartments filled with other young professional tenants, was secure enough to make even Chandra's mother and father sleep easy. No one had front door keys; tenants used a buzzer to gain entry. Inside, a doorman sat in the lobby twenty-four hours a day, checking everyone who came and went. Thirteen surveillance cameras, placed strategically around the building, beamed pictures to screens at the front desk.

Still, Chandra remained careful. Her landlord remembered stopping by the apartment shortly after she moved in. He was accustomed to knocking on doors and having tenants fling them open without even asking who was there. On this occasion he knocked and Chandra asked who was there. With the chain fastened, she then opened the door a crack to speak to the man, who told her he had left something behind in the apartment. Rather than invite the stranger in, she closed the door, went to get the item, then opened the door again and handed it to him. The landlord left impressed with the new tenant's reserve.

Within a week, Chandra reported to the sixth floor of the Bureau of Prisons office near Capitol Hill to begin her internship. Every morning she caught the subway proudly wearing her brand-new credential around her neck. She had been assigned a desk in the public information office, which deals with the media. Her first job was to scour the Internet for stories relating to the nation's ninety-eight federal prisons, after which she prepared a summary for her boss.

Chandra was responsible for typical grunt work such as answering the phones and replying to mail, but she also enjoyed more interesting tasks. One issue looming over the office was the impending execution of the Oklahoma City bomber Timothy McVeigh, and Chandra was given the important duty of coordinating the attendance of reporters and editors at planning sessions for coverage of the event. She also helped process petitions from death row convicts, thereby becoming involved in some of the most crucial functions of the Bureau of Prisons.

When she wasn't working late into the evening at her new job, Chandra jumped enthusiastically into the life of the capital city. She arranged to meet Senator Barbara Boxer from California for breakfast and managed to get a photo for her scrapbook. She gloried in the number of restaurants that catered to vegetarians. On weekends, she and Jennifer explored the monuments and museums.

One day they heard that CNN was assembling an audience at Georgetown University to discuss one of the vice-presidential debates. Chandra finagled tickets and convinced Jennifer to ask a question in front of the cameras. The two laughed and talked about their brush with fame the entire evening.

Spending Election Day 2000 in the highly charged atmosphere of Washington was an experience Chandra would never forget. She and Jennifer met after work and then walked to the Hawk and Dove, a famous watering hole frequented by many politicians. The first election returns were coming in. Already it shaped up to be a nail-biter, and the excited talk in the Hawk and Dove was of nothing else.

Blissfully, the two women soaked it all in, joining in the heated arguments and banter for hours. Then they headed for the Xando coffee bar, a popular hangout for young government workers.

At midnight, with the election still hanging in the balance, Chandra and Jennifer strolled down the Mall and paused in front of the magnificently floodlit Capitol, where they gazed up at the dome in silence for a minute.

Finally Chandra breathed, "Wow!"

****

As they marveled at the wonders of Washington, D.C., Chandra and Jennifer progressively became less awed by their surroundings and attempted to land more permanent employment. They began dropping into congressional offices to meet staffers, make friends, and scout out job prospects. They called these outings "political field trips."

One day in October, they walked unannounced into the offices of Representative Gary Condit, their hometown congressman, in the impressive marbled Rayburn House

Office Building. For Condit, it was the best of times since he expected to be reelected in a few weeks to a seventh term in the House. Thanks in great part to his conservative leanings, he was also being talked about as a possible member of the cabinet if George W. Bush became president.

Condit, pleased at the attention of two young and attractive women on any day, greeted Chandra and Jennifer warmly. He chatted about life back home in Modesto and then insisted on escorting the women to the House Gallery to witness a vote. Afterwards, he brought them back to his office. The wall behind the congressman's imposing desk was covered with framed pictures of himself, none of which included his wife.

Condit then insisted the three of them all pose for a photo together. He led the young women to an area decorated with a Blue Dog painting, symbolic of his position as a leader of a moderate-conservative group in Congress called the Blue Dog Democrats. He invited Chandra to stand on his right and Jennifer on his left, casually placing a hand on both of their shoulders to draw them closer. Condit had no need to tell them to smile as a staff member snapped a picture.

Before they left, Jennifer took the opportunity to ask about available positions, and landed a job as an intern. And somehow, in a move so subtle that not even Jennifer noticed, Gary Condit asked Chandra if he could see her again.

CHAPTER 6

Every year, hundreds of young women with dreams of a job at the political center of the world flock to Washington from all over America, and each fresh crop of starry-eyed interns provides new prey for unscrupulous older politicians on the prowl.

The scandal Chandra Levy would soon fall into with Congressman Condit was by no means unique.

Adultery is a tradition in Washington as old as the capital itself.

"Adultery is the number one problem in the Senate and the House — I'd say seventy to eighty percent of them cheat," said former U.S. Congressman John LeBoutillier, breaking a code of silence that long protected the political elite.

"The feeling among the boys on the Hill is that many of these girls are looking to snag a congressman. The truth is that many of the congressmen take advantage of the girls' naivete. The interns are intoxicated by the desire to be a part of the Washington power base, and power in the form of an older congressman or senator is irresistible."

Some interns soon find something that makes up for their minimal pay checks: the thrill of stealing illicit hours of intimacy with married politicians who are easily old enough to be their fathers.

Chuck Concini, a former aide to Senator Gaylord Nelson, recalled, "You'd sit around the Press Gallery and listen to the old guys talking about which senator was playing around, and what went on in the hideaway offices these guys have."

In Washington, the sexual dance between powerful men and the young women they so smoothly hypnotize even has its ritual trysting places — the Red River Grill, the Tune Inn, and the Capital Grill.

A former Washington intern who experienced it all up close and personal gave this explanation, "You'd think these guys would be running scared now with all the sexual harassment laws. But nothing has changed. When I was an intern we'd go to a weekly ritual called 'the Cocktail Party,' a bash with plenty of food and drink thrown by lobbyists for the congressmen and their staffs they wanted to influence.

"We interns went because we didn't make much money, or made none at all, and we were hungry. Some of the legislators we met were hungry too, but not for food. Their main interest was hitting on the young girls.

"I met a House member at one Cocktail Party who offered me a paid job writing his newsletters. After I started working for him I began to wonder why I was getting paid more than some of his other permanent staffers. Well, I found out after a couple of weeks when the congressman made a pass at me inside the Capitol. I rebuffed him . . . and he fired me the next day."

"To be an intern in Washington is the chance of a life-time," sermonized the well-known Rabbi Samuel M. Stahl.

"Every June and September a new crop of twenty-some-things arrives in our nation's capital. Most of them will be working for government officials who are now in their fifties and sixties. Both the interns and the bosses face the same challenge, which is loneliness.

"These elected officials in many cases are hundreds, if not thousands, of miles away from their families. Yet they are still expected to project the image of family together-ness. They must work long and arduous hours in a city rife with political intrigue. They are also keenly aware that their position is secure only until the next election.

"The interns also feel lonely, rootless and unsettled in a strange and often unwelcoming community. These interns harbor dreams of influence and power. They are vulnerable to the wiles of an older charmer. The politicians, well into middle age, are similarly flattered by the attention of their young, nubile subordinates.

"Thus, both the interns and their bosses confront the same temptation of a romantic relationship they believe will be short. They are also fairly confident it will go unde-tected by family members and the public in general."

"Once they'd met, what followed was inevitable," con-cluded psychiatrist Lieberman regarding Chandra and Condit, both of whom brought sordid personal histories into the risk-laden mix. If two individuals were meant to uphold Washington's tradition of adultery, these were the prime candidates to do it.

"In the first minute their eyes locked onto each other, she saw the challenge of a powerful daddy — the most power-ful she'd ever encountered — to be won away from his wife and any other girlfriends he might have. Gary was a real prize, and she instantly saw him as a long-lasting trophy she might turn into a husband.

"Condit saw her as a trophy too — but no more than a temporary sexual trophy. When he looked at Chandra, he saw easy prey. She was vulnerable, an easy conquest for a man so accomplished in conquering women. And the more smitten she became, the easier it would be.

"In his mind he was thinking, 'She'll do whatever I want. I can turn her into my sex slave.'"

CHAPTER 7

For their first date — although neither of them called it that — Chandra and Condit agreed to meet for dinner at the aptly named Tryst coffeehouse and restaurant, on 18th Street in Adams Morgan, not far from Gary's condo. If the walls could talk, they might have tipped Chandra off to the fact that she was by no means the first attractive young woman the congressman had brought there.

That dinner was the first and probably the last normal, open rendezvous she would be allowed to enjoy with her lover. Henceforth their affair was to be a thing of absolute secrecy, a frustrating mix of cloak-and-dagger deception, intrigue, denials, furtive sex, dedicated phone numbers, codes, and even disguises. No more cozy conversations over coffee in front of everyone at Tryst, no introductions to his friends, no boasting to her girlfriends about her new man.

Perhaps most bizarre of all, Condit forbade Chandra from carrying any identification when they met.

These became the Condit Rules that he insisted be maintained religiously at all times. Either Chandra went along with them or she was history. She had no way of knowing that they were the same save-his-skin rules that the politician used again and again with one woman after another during decades of philandering.

Chandra was quickly falling deeply in love, and if happiness meant doing things this way, she could accept that. He was a powerful politician, after all, with understandable security concerns. In what would become a pattern, she rationalized what others would see as more than unusual.

Condit was the answer to the prayers of a girl who had always been dazzled by older, powerful men. How insignificant her policeman and doctor lovers must suddenly have seemed in comparison.

Only Gary Condit knows the nuances of their relationship now, but details have emerged little by little in the veiled accounts Chandra revealed to two key people: her forty-one-year-old aunt, Linda Zamsky, and Sven Jones, a Bureau of Prisons colleague who worked out with her at the gym and became her confidante and shoulder to cry on. In general, she steadfastly kept quiet about her steamy love affair, but eventually she had to talk about the burning secret in her life.

"It was clear without a doubt that they were involved in an intimate relationship," said Zamsky firmly. Linda, like Sven, opened up to the media in the hope of shedding light on what might have happened to Chandra. "She described in vivid detail some of their bedroom encounters."

"When they were together, it was pretty intense," Jones told reporter Lisa DePaulo. "That was a given."

One night after their fateful first meeting at Tryst, Condit invited Chandra into a more intimate setting. She took a taxi to Condit's condo in Adams Morgan, waited for an empty elevator, as she had been specifically instructed, and knocked nervously on the door of his apartment on the top floor of the five-story building. Condit breezily showed her around the spacious living room, small den, single bedroom, and kitchen. Then they made love for the first of many times.

Soon Chandra was spending entire weekends at Condit's place, sharing chocolate-chip-cookie-dough ice cream she bought on her way to see him. It became one of their traditions, romantically feeding each other heaping spoonfuls. Then they gave each other sensual full-body oil massages. Her vastly more experienced lover introduced her to places on the far shores of sexuality she had never visited before.

"Pure sexual pleasure was more important to him than her," explained psychiatrist Carole Lieberman. "Sex to Chandra was an affirmation of her attractiveness. Every time Gary Condit made love to her, she felt validated as a woman.

"She felt sexy, pretty, and powerful because she was stealing him away from all the other women he could undoubtedly have," Lieberman continued. "She's triumphant, thinking to herself, 'This man can't resist me.' The more powerful or attractive the man is to other women, the more the woman who is actually with him feels her self-esteem boosted. She's got him — and the others haven't.

"Chandra probably did things in bed with Gary that she'd never done before and hadn't necessarily wanted to do. He was taking her into a realm of wild sex she'd never known. It was experimental sex for her, and some of it was exciting. Subconsciously she would enjoy doing things her family would think were naughty.

"But she was also proving to him what a devoted love slave she could be, and why he should marry her. She would have done anything he asked if it meant keeping him."

The trouble was that after a month, Chandra wanted to tell someone. But the Condit Rules had kept her lips sealed. Whoever she confided in, it needed to be someone she trusted totally to keep her secrets.

Chandra turned to Aunt Linda, married to her uncle, Paul Zamsky, for eight years. From the time Linda joined the family, the two women had engaged in girl talk. Whereas Chandra, like so many other young women, never felt comfortable sharing the details of her sex life with her mother, she opened up to Aunt Linda, who always gave her unquestioning support. During a family reunion in Florida, Chandra even told Linda about her love for the Modesto cop, Mark Steele.

When Chandra arrived in Washington in September, before she met Condit, one of her first calls was to Aunt Linda.

"She said, 'Hey Lynn, I'm out on the East Coast — when can we get together?'" Linda recalled, smiling at the fond memory. "We chitchatted on the phone, nothing significant that I can remember, just girl talk. She was excited about her job. Being here in Washington was something she'd dreamed about for quite a while. Working in a government position was something she'd wanted to do. So she felt that she was on her way to where she wanted her career to take her."

But Chandra found herself so busy with her duties at the Bureau of Prisons and the rest of her life that the first time she and Linda finally got together was over the Thanksgiving holiday. Two days earlier, Chandra had called and announced happily, "I have a lot to tell you about . . . a lot has happened here in Washington."

The words were casual, but her tone was enough to pique Linda's interest. Perhaps anticipating her aunt's next question, Chandra quickly added, "I can't talk. No — I'll talk to you when I get there."

Chandra caught a commuter train from the city and Linda went to pick her up at the Perryville station on November 22nd, the Wednesday night before Thanksgiving. Chandra's grandmother was at the house, also, and the two younger women waited until she had gone to bed to get down to the real conversation.

"We had our girl talk, and that's where she first mentioned she was dating a man that was married and quite a few years older than her," explained Linda. "There was a look in her eyes. She was excited. I said, 'Well, how old?' She said he was 'fiftyish.' And I said, 'Well, who is he?'"

"He's married," Chandra repeated slowly, torn between the Condit Rules and her longing to proudly pour out her heart to Linda about the man she was falling in love with.

At first, the Condit Rules prevailed.

"He's here in Washington and he goes home occasionally . . . He's in the government and he has two kids."

Chandra was totally smitten, Linda realized. Her face glowed as she spoke about him.

"She said it was a new relationship — she'd been dating him for four to six weeks prior to Thanksgiving," recalled Linda.

They kissed goodnight and went to bed with Linda no closer to learning the identity of Chandra's mystery man.

The house was full for Thanksgiving Day, and they never found a chance to talk alone. The following Friday morning, they took Chandra's grandmother to the local mall. Later they settled in comfortably for more girl talk.

"I asked her, 'How do you get in touch with him if he is so secretive about this relationship?' She said, 'Well . . .' and this is when she accidentally said his name out loud to me. She said she would dial a phone number, it would play music and she would leave a message. Or [she said] 'I would call the office and they'd answer, "Congressman Gary Condit's office."'"

Chandra's hands suddenly flew up to her mouth. "Oops!" she exclaimed, panic in her voice. "You didn't hear that, did you?"

"I said, 'no,'" Linda explained. "And of course I did, but I made light of it. I kind of dummied up because I wanted her to feel comfortable. I didn't want her to be a nervous wreck talking about her boyfriend. Obviously, I was one of the few people that she could talk to about this, so I wanted her to feel comfortable. So she said his name and then continued with how she would get in touch with him."

Now that the floodgates were opened, Chandra poured out to her aunt all the details of the romance that she had been keeping to herself for weeks. Blushing happily, she revealed that she and Gary were already lovers.

"She said he would call her back after she would leave a message," Linda said. "She was very patient."

Not surprisingly, that undemanding patience was something Condit found highly attractive in Chandra. Early on in their close relationship, she told her aunt, he had paid her a telling compliment:

"It's nice to see someone that's willing to be flexible with my schedule and my lifestyle. You know, I haven't had that in a relationship before."

The words hung in the air between aunt and niece.

"I haven't had that in a relationship before . . ."

Chandra did not elaborate, but Linda realized that her niece had accepted the reality that she was not the first extramarital lover in this politician's life. Condit had told Chandra she was free to date other men, she confided, trying to justify his own views on "open relationships," but she would have none of it.

"She wanted this to be a monogamous relationship," added Linda, examining her niece's early commitment. "She was willing to do whatever he wanted her to do in order for this relationship to work."

Linda asked Chandra what she and Condit actually did together, considering that every meeting had to be so secretive. Chandra explained that her lover was busy most of the time with his political career, attending a lot of luncheons, dinners, and benefits in Washington.

"When we're together we just like to hang out at his place and spend time together," she said happily. "We can cook in or we'll go get a bite to eat."

If they ate out, it was at Chinese or Thai restaurants hidden in the suburbs, far from Capitol Hill where he was less likely to be recognized.

"How do you go out in public together if your affair is such a secret?" Linda asked. The answer, she recalled, took her breath away.

"Chandra said they would take a taxi. She would come out the door, grab the taxi, and then he would come out in a baseball cap, jacket — kind of a little incognito — and get in the cab with her. I asked if he was afraid the cabbie was going to know who he was? She said no, they didn't do a lot of talking in the cab. They kept everything very quiet.

"And these were the rules that she had to follow for this relationship to be all right. He wanted no one to know about this. He was emphatic — it had to remain secret. If anybody found out about this relationship, it was done. Over. Kaput. If she couldn't keep a secret, there would be no relationship.

"When she went to his apartment [building], if someone was in the elevator or got in with her, she was to push the button for another floor. She could not get off on Condit's floor. If someone asked her, 'Oh, you look new in the building, did you just move in?' she had to say, 'No — I'm not new here. I'm visiting a sick friend.'

"These were all little details that she had worked out with him that really showed how serious this relationship was — and how serious it was that it had to remain a secret."

Later that Friday evening at her aunt's house, Chandra insisted on turning the television station to watch a cable channel's broadcast of a congressional session, and she explained to Linda the various functions of senators and congressmen. She was taken with the process of government and excited at her new role within it.

"I don't remember if Condit ever came up on TV," Linda said. "I don't believe he did, because she would have gotten a little bit more excited, and then I would have seen what he looked like."

However, between the speeches, Chandra was more than happy to give her Aunt Linda a description of her man.

"She described him as looking a little bit like Harrison Ford. She said he was lean, in good shape, worked out, was very conscientious about his body for fifty-three years old." Linda made a mental note, trying to visualize the mystery man. "I already knew he was 'fiftyish' — but she said fifty-three."

Chandra said that her man rode a Harley, just like Linda's husband, Paul. He was apparently quite the motorcycle buff, biking around the country to rallies. But when Linda suggested that maybe in the spring they should all take a trip together, Chandra demurred.

"He would never do that, because he wouldn't want to be seen," she admitted. "Paul might know him, or you might — it's just not something he would do."

By the time Chandra was getting ready to return to Washington at the end of the holiday weekend, Linda felt comfortable enough with the secret to offer her niece and her lover a chance to get away together. Linda wanted Chandra to be happy, and if her niece needed this relationship to work, she would help.

"I said, 'If you want to come out here and spend the weekend, you're more than welcome. You two can go upstairs and have your privacy. It'll be your own little bed and breakfast and you don't have to see me at all if you just want to get away and be together.'"

Chandra never took her aunt up on the offer. The Condit Rules forced her into blind submission, and she accepted a life of secrecy that most people would never agree to. For Chandra, a normal and open romance would never occur.

"She told me she didn't make plans for anything, because she wanted to wait to hear from him," said Linda. "This was how she ran her life."

CHAPTER 8

Chandra resisted telling even her best friend in Washington, Jennifer Baker, about the affair with Congressman Gary Condit. In November 2000, and again in an e-mail around New Year's Day, Chandra mentioned a "new boyfriend," but she said only that the man was an agent for the FBI.

"She didn't tell me much about him — it just didn't seem important at the time," recalled Jennifer.

Imagine how intrigued the Condit office intern would have been had she known that her pal's secret lover was her boss!

The FBI connection was not completely random. Chandra had found that she enjoyed her law enforcement work so much that she set her sights on joining the agency when her internship at the Bureau of Prisons concluded. She had already submitted an official application for an analyst's job.

Chandra visited Condit's office half a dozen times after her friend went to work there. But there were always plausible reasons — be it for lunch with Jennifer, a request for White House tour tickets, or schedules of Capitol Hill events.

It was enough of a smokescreen to confuse all but the weary veteran staffers who'd seen it all before — and it didn't matter if they knew because they operated under Condit Rules of silence themselves.

It was not until April 2001 that Chandra's mother, Susan Levy, finally learned about the affair.

"She didn't tell me who she was involved with," revealed Susan. "I kinda got it out of her. She told me she couldn't tell me his name — that I would eventually understand. I asked her, 'Is it Gary Condit?'

"How did you know?" gasped Chandra.

"Mother's intuition," Susan replied gently.

"She asked me to keep it secret. I didn't even say anything to my husband, because I tried to honor that. She repeated that I would eventually understand."

For months, both parents had been suspicious, privately wondering how Chandra managed to obtain a seat in the VIP section at the inauguration of President George W. Bush and dance at one of the balls.

For Susan, it was becoming clear — Chandra had more than just a contact.

Susan realized she had missed other clues. For one thing, on a visit home, Chandra, who had always been a rock 'n' roll fan, taped some of Frank Sinatra's most romantic numbers, like "Fly Me to the Moon."

Later, her daughter admitted that the Sinatra song was one of Condit's favorites, a tune that they had shared and made their own.

Then Susan read a newspaper article about Gary Condit that noted he's a teetotaler. Chandra had mentioned that her mysterious new boyfriend in Washington didn't touch alcohol of any kind.

Not long afterwards, Susan recounted a conversation she claimed she had with a local Pentecostal minister named Otis Thomas. Although Thomas would later deny the conversation ever took place, Susan claimed it sent chills down her spine and sent her rushing to the phone to issue a warning to Chandra.

The minister, who was also the Levys' gardener, was tending the freshly blooming roses in the Levys' backyard when Susan brought him a cold drink and they began to talk. Thomas asked how Chandra was getting on in Washington, said Susan, who then impulsively confided that Chandra had become friends with the local congressman, Gary Condit.

She asked Thomas if he ever heard anything about Condit and any other women, and according to Susan the question unlocked a flood of secrets hidden in the minister's heart for seven years. In 1994, his own daughter Jennifer, only 18 at the time, had asked her father for advice on how to go about breaking off a relationship with a man that had gone sour, Susan said.

When he asked Jennifer the name of the man, Susan said, the girl told him it was Congressman Condit and she had met him at a political rally.

Thomas advised Jennifer to end the liaison with Condit immediately, Susan recalled, and she took his suggestion.

Susan said she then confessed to Thomas that Chandra and Condit where also more than friends.

"Tell her to end the relationship right away," was the advice Susan remembered receiving from Thomas.

Susan raced to the phone in her home and called Chandra in Washington. She told her daughter about the conversation she said she had with Thomas. She urged Chandra "to be very careful."

Her daughter told her to mind her own business. She was a grown woman. She could deal with it.

✳✳✳✳✳✳✳✳✳✳✳✳

In early January 2001, Chandra was convinced that she and Condit had a bright future together. When Aunt Linda called her one day that month, Chandra said she might possibly move in with her lover. It made sense, she said, because it would save her money, and she could look after his apartment and be there whenever he needed her. Next, Chandra called her landlord and sounded him out about breaking her lease. She was thinking about moving in with her boyfriend, she told him.

By February 1st, those hopes were somehow dashed. Condit must have convinced Chandra to put off such plans. When Chandra and the landlord spoke again, she told him the move was off.

"It didn't work out," Chandra explained.

When it came time for the traditional family Passover gathering in April, Chandra hesitated to commit to joining the Zamskys until the last minute. She wanted to be available to Condit, whose name she no longer tried to conceal from her aunt. In the end, Condit was busy and Chandra went to the Zamskys.

She arrived at the Perryville station on the evening of April 5, 2001, and was picked up by her aunt. Again, she took care not to mention Condit in front of other relatives. But the next morning, while her grandmother and uncle still slept, she and Aunt Linda went into gossip mode.

"She showed me the bracelet on her right wrist, a gold

bracelet. A chain bracelet, a very nice piece of jewelry, double clasp, and she said Condit bought it for her."

In addition to the elegant bracelet, Chandra revealed, Condit had given her a box of Godiva chocolates on Valentine's Day and airline tickets for trips back to California. She in turn gave him an expensive silk tie from the exclusive Thomas Pink shop for his fifty-fourth birthday on April 21st.

Chandra shared enough bedroom secrets for Linda to realize her niece was now involved in a torrid affair. The couple had sex at least two or three times a week at Condit's apartment. Chandra would go there straight from work or the health club, often carrying her gym bag or backpack.

Linda Zamsky gave her only one piece of gentle advice: "Don't put all your eggs in one basket — he's a married man."

As if to counter any doubts, Chandra confided to her aunt that she and Condit had already discussed their future in detail. They planned to carry on their affair in secret for exactly five years, at which time Condit would quit Congress, leave his wife, marry Chandra, and then she would have his baby.

When Aunt Linda pointed out that by then Condit would be nearly sixty, and that was not the best age to father a child, Chandra just smiled.

"Children today can adjust to the things going on," she said soothingly.

The Five-Year Plan, Chandra called it.

CHAPTER 9

Gary Condit had always been supremely confident of his ability to juggle his girlfriends, his wife, and also politics. But Chandra Levy would prove to be different from all of his former lovers. Ever since she was a little girl, Chandra had impressed everyone with her refusal to take no for an answer when facing a challenge. And by early 2001, she had set her sights on becoming Mrs. Gary Condit.

The Five-Year Plan now seemed ponderous and far too distant. Chandra was becoming increasingly impatient. In the first ten days of April, she called Condit's secret phone number seven times. Her phone records trace a pattern of a casual romance boiling over into deep obsession.

Sven Jones, her close friend, said that around this time Chandra wanted to talk about nothing but Congressman Condit and how to get him to leave his wife.

"Chandra could be a pretty forward person," recalled Jones. "She was not the type of woman who was going to be the little mistress waiting at home on the couch." The tormented intern, he explained, "vacillated between being angry with him and feeling somewhat placated by him."

"I tried to tell her," Jones continued, "that if you push a man like that too hard, he's going to feel as if he's lost some self-control. I said, 'If you really want to hook this guy, you should lie low and let him feel like he's making the decisions.'"

"I've invested too much in this," she told him flatly.

"She was gathering up the courage to ask for an exclusive relationship," said Jones.

It had been a long and frustrating cold winter for Chandra. Despite her determination to fit in with whatever Condit wanted, she often felt lonely and abandoned. In one telephone conversation with Aunt Linda, she lamented about spending hours by herself at his empty apartment, waiting for him to return. She didn't know what to do to fill the time, and asked for some advice.

"What's the apartment like?" Linda asked.

Looking around the sparse one-bedroom bachelor pad, Chandra replied, "Well, he grows cactus."

"Well, get a terrarium," suggested her aunt cheerfully, still trying to help Chandra make the most of the situation. "Go to a craft shop, get some colored sand, get little cactus and plant them in the terrarium."

When Chandra didn't seem impressed with the idea, Linda tried another. "Organize his closet," she said.

"It's pretty clean," replied Chandra forlornly, pacing the room slowly from one end to the other.

"Well, color-coordinate everything in there. You know, put all the long-sleeve shirts by color."

At least the conversation passed some time.

Her friends believe that by now Chandra had convinced herself that she wasn't just "another woman" intent on breaking up a man's marriage and home. She rationalized her feelings by telling herself that Carolyn and Condit lived 3,000 miles apart. Besides, Condit had claimed that his wife suffered from "encephalitis of the brain," and was unable to give him much attention. What kind of marriage was that?

Yet every time she broached the issue with her man, he managed to sweet-talk her back to the status quo.

"She wanted a commitment from him and she was pushing him in the last few months," noted the reporter Lisa DePaulo. "It was not because she was some manipulative woman, because she wasn't. She believed what he said. Chandra didn't want to be his only mistress; she wanted to be his only woman. And she would force the confrontation, and then he would charm her.

"One of her friends told me, 'I really worried what would happen if he stopped placating her.'"

✳✳✳✳✳✳✳✳✳✳✳✳

Any number of experts in psychology and human relationships have analyzed the predicament Chandra found herself in. They all believe her hopes and dreams were unrealistic, except to the headstrong young woman herself. The chance that they could have lived happily ever after was more remote than hitting the Lotto.

"Male politicians can be very narcissistic and like to think they're always in control, which is why so many of them have affairs with much younger women," said forensic psychologist Reid Meloy, author of *Violent Attachments*.

"But if the woman isn't compliant, she can get herself into trouble. It's plausible that when a young woman argues with that kind of personality, she could trigger violence."

The popular crime writer Ann Rule, who is a former police officer, researched just such a situation for her bestseller, *And Never Let Go*.

It was the tragic story of another younger woman, Anne Marie Fahey — bright and intelligent, like Chandra — who was also drawn toward politics as the trusted secretary of the governor of Delaware. Anne Marie vanished in June 1996, at the age of thirty. Months later, her married lover, a wealthy and successful forty-nine-year-old attorney, was arrested for her murder and eventually sentenced to death.

"These young women are in no way equipped to deal with the seduction of the older charming man with power who makes them feel they're special," explained Rule. "They have no idea how many other women there have been before them — or that they are interchangeable."

Richard Tuch, author of *The Single Woman-Married Man Syndrome*, added, "In the end these liaisons are tumultuous for everybody involved. The relationship goes through a series of cycles, during which the participants swing from feeling great about the relationship to feeling terrible about what they're being put through.

"But regardless of how hellish things become, neither partner seems able to break off the relationship."

Chandra no doubt would have smiled smugly and informed all the experts in the world that they were wrong this time.

She and Condit had something special.

CHAPTER 10

A party to celebrate Chandra's birthday on April 14th was held at the familiar home of Aunt Linda. Chandra blew out the twenty-four candles on a chocolate cake decorated with flowers and the inscription, "Happy Birthday, Chandra. We Love You."

On a family video taken that day, Susan Levy, who had come east for the occasion with her husband Bob, joked about the weather outside.

"Wherever Chandra goes, there are usually interesting storms."

Her father persuaded Chandra to read a birthday card out loud, and with a sigh she agreed. In a soft voice, she read:

"May a day of sunny hours start a year of dreams come true."

As she finished, lightning flashed ominously outside.

"Kaboom!" exclaimed her father.

For the first time in a family situation, Chandra talked animatedly about her "guy," although she was careful not to divulge his name or occupation.

"She was very much in love and had stars in her eyes," recalled her godmother, Fran Iseman.

A week later, Chandra was hit by a bombshell. In casual conversation with a personnel officer at the Bureau of Prisons, she mentioned that she had managed to graduate from USC early — the previous December — although on her application for the internship she had stated that she did not expect to complete her master's degree until May 2001. Taken aback, the staff member pointed out that government regulations demand that internships end within 120 days of graduation.

Chandra had expected to stay at the Bureau of Prisons job until September. Instead, her internship was abruptly canceled. Her last day, she was told, would be the following Monday, April 23rd.

With the part of her life that had kept her close to Condit suddenly and unexpectedly over, Chandra was distraught. She had applied for the analyst's job at the FBI a month earlier, but heard nothing. Now the future of their relationship took on a new urgency.

On the morning of Tuesday, April 24th, seventeen hours after saying goodbye to friends at the Bureau of Prisons, Chandra headed for Condit's apartment.

It was their last meeting, said Condit, and it lasted an hour and a half. Questioned later, he refused to admit or deny that they had sex that morning. He said only that despite the job disappointment, Chandra was upbeat. They talked about her plans to return to California by train. There were no tears when they parted.

"We were friends, and the friendship was going to continue," he insisted. "There was never a thought that we weren't going to stay in contact or see each other."

If Chandra truly was "upbeat," as Condit claimed, she

managed to maintain optimism despite further frustrations. On top of everything else, Chandra learned to her dismay that there would be no chance for her to meet Condit again for at least nine days. Condit's wife was about to make one of her visits to Washington.

Carolyn Condit flew into Washington's Reagan Airport around 7:30 p.m. on April 28th. She and her husband were driven by a staff member to the apartment in Adams Morgan that had so recently been Chandra's love nest. Carolyn planned to go to Bethesda Naval Medical Center in the Maryland suburbs, attend a luncheon for congressional wives hosted by First Lady Laura Bush, and stay in town with her husband until May 3rd.

The same night that Carolyn arrived in the city, Chandra e-mailed her landlord at 11:14 p.m.

"It looks like my plans have suddenly changed. I was just informed this week that my job appointment time is up, so I am out of work now. I am going back to California for my graduation during the week of May 8, and I'm moving back there for good . . . I would like to vacate the apartment on May 5 or 6 if possible. I really hate giving up the apartment, but I think I need to be in California for a while to figure out what my next move is."

Condit and Chandra last spoke to each other, the congressman claimed, on the following day, Sunday, April 29th, when Condit returned a call from his mistress. He said he asked her when she was leaving Washington, and she told him it would be in the next few days. She would call him from California, she promised.

By his recollection, it could not have been a more casual conversation, but it obviously meant a good deal more to Chandra — afterward she called Aunt Linda and left a brief message on her answering machine.

"I have some really big news," Chandra announced cheerfully. "Call me."

Linda will regret forever that she did not return the call quickly enough.

Telephone company records show that Chandra tried to call Condit five more times in the two days before she vanished, despite knowing he was probably with Carolyn.

On April 30th at 7:26 p.m., she walked into the Washington Sports Club on Connecticut Avenue. She had started using the club more regularly when her romance with Condit grew stronger.

"She told me, 'I want to keep my upper body in tone — it makes me feel very good about myself to be lean and muscular," said one of the people at the gym with whom she became friendly.

"She wore baggy white or pink T-shirts and knee-length stretch pants for her workout, and she was never flirtatious or suggestive. She wasn't the type of girl who went to the club looking to pick up guys or get dates. She wasn't wild or anything — she was very methodical about things and always seemed to know exactly what she was doing.

"She was her normal, jubilant self. You know, 'healthy body, healthy mind' is just what she was." The friend recalled that during her final visit to the club, Chandra had asked to cancel her membership. "She told me, 'I'm moving out of the neighborhood. I'm going home to California.'"

Chandra stayed until 8:30 p.m.

She was, according to the friend, "The same as always, very upbeat, very friendly, always smiling."

CHAPTER 11

Bob and Susan Levy last spoke to Chandra on the phone on Friday, April 27, 2001. On Tuesday, May 1st, they received a final e-mail that was nothing more than the forwarding of an airline's list of supersaver fares between Modesto and Los Angeles. The Levys were planning to fly to L.A. for their daughter's graduation ceremony at USC on May 11th, and she obviously thought they might be looking for flight bargains.

When they did not hear from Chandra for a few more days, growing increasingly worried, they called her home and left one frantic message after another, eventually filling her voicemail to capacity. By Saturday, May 5th, their worry had intensified into gut-wrenching fear. Bob Levy decided it was time to contact authorities in Washington, D.C.

After they frantically begged the police to go to Chandra's apartment and check things out, an officer agreed.

The police never called back.

The next day, Bob and Susan, certain they were getting the brush-off from the District of Columbia Police Department, tried again. This time an officer called back several hours later, but his news told the Levys nothing. Police had been to the apartment, he said, but Chandra was not there. He never mentioned the packed suitcases or anything else about the state of the apartment.

Later that Sunday, Susan instinctively knew whom they had to call next. Bob picked up the phone and dialed the home number of Congressman Condit in nearby Ceres. Condit was home for the weekend, but Carolyn answered. Her husband was out, watching his two grandsons take part in a tae kwon do demonstration. One can only imagine what went through Condit's mind when he returned home and his wife told him that a constituent, a Dr. Robert Levy, had called to say his daughter Chandra was missing in Washington and he needed help from his congressman.

Condit eventually returned the call, and he immediately heard the panic in the doctor's voice.

"Just the tone of his voice sent chills running down my spine," Condit said later, claiming dire concern. "It made me really fearful that something might have happened to her."

Bob's version of the conversation is far different. According to him, after he informed Condit that Chandra was missing, the congressman's response was, "Oh."

****

On Monday, Susan Levy decided to go through Chandra's cell phone bill, which the couple always paid. Studying the list of calls, she was struck by how often a certain Washington number she didn't recognize appeared.

Curious, she dialed the number and heard what she described as, "airy, romantic music."

Over the music came a recorded voice with instructions for the caller to punch in his or her own phone number, which Susan did. Unwittingly, she had stumbled on the pager that was Chandra and Condit's "secret number."

Although she would not admit it even to herself, Susan had known in her heart whose number it would prove to be, and she was not surprised when Gary Condit called later, answering her page. He was already back in D.C.

The conversation started off awkwardly, and then Susan forced herself to bring the burning question on her mind to her lips. She gathered all the nerve she possessed, and asked him point-blank, "Congressman Condit, are you having an affair with my daughter, and do you know where she is?"

Tough-skinned as he was, the veteran politician must have been shaken, but he kept his composure. "No," he replied crisply. Susan recalled his tone as being matter-of-fact.

Then, Susan remembered, he explained soothingly, "I'm only professionally involved with your daughter. I regard her highly. I respect her as a personal friend, and I only have a professional relationship with her."

"What do you mean by that?" she asked.

Condit replied that Chandra had asked him about law school and the FBI, and that he advised her to learn a second language such as Spanish, which would help in her career.

Susan pressed on bravely.

"She called you awfully late. There are calls at ten o'clock at night."

"And he says," recalled Susan, "'Oh, we work late in the

evenings in the office up at Capitol Hill, and we get many calls late at night.' That's the way he answered me."

During the phone call, Susan never told Condit she knew he was lying. She had, after all, already learned of her daughter's intimate relationship with the congressman. Instead, during a conversation that became increasingly tense, she asked him to help roust the D.C. police into action. The cops did not seem to believe the Levys when they said there was something terribly ominous about Chandra's silence.

Condit told Susan that a member of his staff had called the police and FBI earlier that morning to report that a constituent was missing.

Again, authorities promised action.

Yet nothing happened for another three days, and the delay may have been crucial. By the time the police finally went to Chandra's apartment again on May 10th, the videotape in the camera in the lobby that recorded the arrival and departure of visitors on May 1st, the day she disappeared, had been taped over.

The first police officers to enter the apartment on May 10th found two travel bags almost completely packed, but clothes still on hangers. A laptop was plugged in and open on the desk. Chandra's cell phone; checkbook; and a wallet full of credit cards, cash, and identification, including her driver's license, sat nearby. Jewelry, including a gold necklace, diamond stud earrings, and a gold ankle bracelet, was in a drawer. In the bathroom, they found makeup and toiletries. In the kitchen, the refrigerator was bare except for pasta leftovers and several of Chandra's favorite Reese's peanut butter cups. Dirty dishes were in the sink.

Her running shoes were lying on the floor. A comforter had been dumped in the small hallway, apparently after having been washed and dried in a laundry room down the hall from her apartment. Later, investigators would see that as a major clue to the timing of her disappearance.

Police originally thought Chandra left her apartment after logging off her computer. But they now wondered: Did she wash and dry the comforter after surfing the net?

If so, she left much later in the afternoon.

In a gray kitchen cabinet, authorities found among the plates and cups a coffee mug printed with the following:

Odds of meeting a single man — 1 in 23;

Odds of meeting a cute single man — 1 in 529;

Odds of meeting a cute, single and smart man — 1 in 3,245,873;

Odds of meeting the above when you look your best — 1 in 9,729,528.

CHAPTER 12

C ondit chose that day, May 10th, to make his first public statement about the missing intern whose face was now all over the morning papers and TV news shows. He called Chandra "a great person and a good friend," and he announced that he would contribute $10,000 to a reward fund.

"We hope she is found safe and sound," he concluded.

The *Modesto Bee* reported that Jennifer Thomas, the daughter of minister Otis Thomas, shouted, "That's a lie," at the television set when she heard those words.

She had just heard of Chandra's disappearance and knew something wasn't right, according to published reports.

Although the minister would later recant his statement, he initially reported that Jennifer became more and more shaken. Finally, she told him Condit had warned her after they'd broken up never to tell anyone about the affair.

The Levys reported Jennifer's alleged involvement with Condit to the FBI and agent Todd Irinaga interviewed her father.

Thomas reportedly promised to help get his daughter to cooperate. But Jennifer suddenly went into hiding, leaving behind a note on her front door for reporters.

"I never met that congressman who's involved in all this. I don't even know how both me and my father got mixed up in all this."

To this day, Susan Levy is convinced Thomas and his daughter were frightened off by Condit forces.

****

Desperate, the Levy family turned to the Carole Sund-Carrington Memorial Reward Foundation. The foundation had been set up by Carole Carrington and her husband in the wake of one of northern California's most horrendous tragedies. In 1999, their forty-two-year-old daughter, Carole Sund; her fifteen-year-old daughter Juli; and six-teen-year-old Silvina Pelosso, who was visiting the family from Argentina, disappeared and were later found brutally murdered.

The Carringtons, trying to make something good come out of something so tragic, set up the foundation to help other families locate missing persons. Susan Levy had considered volunteering for the foundation in the past. Now she found herself needing their help.

The Levys had already offered a reward of $15,000 and eventually would spend more than $200,000 of their own money hiring lawyers and investigators for an independent probe into Chandra's disappearance. But they realized that they needed to use every tool at their disposal. The professionals at Sund-Carrington knew just how to coordinate a media blitz that would get attention and stop memories from fading.

Susan and Bob recognized Condit was receiving the kid-glove treatment from the District of Columbia Police Department that congressmen have come to expect. The police continued to tell them to stay silent and let them handle everything, but the slow progress of the case infuriated the concerned parents. These were, after all, the same officials who had neglected to even call them back initially.

By now, thousands of fliers with the headline MISSING printed over a photograph of Chandra as a teenager were posted by the police all over D.C.

Ironically, a similar picture, one of the glamour shots taken by the fashion photographer Jon Michael Terry when Chandra was seventeen and aspired to become a model, appeared in newspapers around the world as police hunted for her in Washington. Even in their worst nightmares her parents never imagined it would be used for this purpose.

"If they gave me fifty cents for every time that picture was shown, I could retire," said Terry, who has resisted any opportunity to cash in on his work. "But I see all these sharks circling out there, and I don't want to be one of them."

But why was the DCPD distributing photographs that were seven years old?

One of Chandra's friends told detectives that at the time she disappeared she looked a lot different from how she looked in the photo — her hair was shorter and her nose seemed different. The photo was not an accurate resemblance.

"The police told me it was because she had cosmetic surgery to her nose," he said.

So why hadn't they used a more recent photo? The inaccuracies of the official description of Chandra on the police

Web site were also puzzling. It claimed she was 5 feet 4 inches — an inch taller than her true height. It neglected to mention two striking factors that might well have caught someone's eye — the distinctive rose tattoo on her ankle and the three piercings in each ear. Nor did it describe the personalized diamond ring she was believed to be wearing or the key ring she was carrying when she left the apartment.

Those details weren't available when the notice was first posted on May 10th, said police spokesman Sergeant Joe Gentile.

Nevertheless, when this information was provided, the officers responsible for updating the information failed to do so.

As the police continued to blunder onward, Condit was starting to feel heat from other places. On June 8th, in a distinctly unfriendly editorial, the *Modesto Bee* declared that their hometown congressman's "five weeks of silence is enough." Condit had a duty to clarify his relationship with Chandra, the paper urged.

On June 14th, the Levys went public to urge Condit to come clean. When he did nothing, they began inviting camera crews and reporters into their home, handing out sodas and explaining on the air and in print that they needed to know what had happened to their daughter. As visitors walked in the front door, they passed by a portrait of a smiling Chandra and the framed University of Southern California master's degree awarded ten days after her disappearance.

Many of the reporters' questions were personal and painful, but Bob Levy simply shrugged.

"If it helps get her home, I don't care what questions are asked."

When the press corps became too large to invite inside, the Levys started holding daily press conferences on the front lawn.

"Anyway we can do it, we'll do it," explained Susan. "How would you be if you were a parent?"

On June 21st, Susan and Bob Levy were in Washington for consultations with their newly hired attorney, Billy Martin, one of the capital's leading criminal defense lawyers and a former prosecutor. Their goal was to cut through the bureaucratic thicket. Not long before, Martin had represented another person embroiled in a crisis — Monica Lewinsky's mom.

Susan said fiercely, "We're not used to playing with the big folks, but we're just as important as any politician."

Martin shepherded the nervous couple through an emotional televised press conference. Susan clutched a fluffy yellow duck, a memento from their daughter's childhood, as they called on Congressman Condit to cooperate and come forward with any information that might help them find Chandra.

In a new development, they revealed that Condit had called them at home the previous week, but they had declined to talk to him because they thought it was a conversation their lawyer should also hear.

Now they were available, they said.

Evidently, Gary Condit was watching the press conference, and he took the bait. Immediately afterwards, he released a statement that intimated he would meet with the Levys and their attorney.

"Anyone who saw Dr. and Mrs. Levy today," he said in his statement, "cannot but feel their deep concern and worry.

"People following these events know that I met with

police officials as soon as Chandra Levy was reported missing and answered their questions in hopes that any information I had could help find her. Since that time, I have spoken with police again and reached out to Miss Levy's parents. If there is any new information I can provide, I will do so without hesitation."

The couple then met with Police Chief Charles Ramsey and Executive Assistant Police Chief Terrance Gainer. The two senior police officers filled them in on the search for Chandra, but gave them little hope. Afterward, Susan said only that she believed the police were working "very hard."

"We don't know where our daughter is," she added plaintively. "I continue to hope and pray she will come back to us alive."

By the time they returned to their hotel, Condit's statement was on the wires, and one of Billy Martin's assistants had faxed it to the Levys. Initially, the couple could not respond beyond feeling anger at Condit's claim of full cooperation, considering that he had been less than honest regarding his relationship with their daughter.

Martin, however, realized that the statement had exposed a chink in the politician's armor.

He advised Susan and Bob that they should seize the opportunity Condit had perhaps unwittingly given them — it was time to press him on his offer to talk. They agreed, and Martin placed a call to Abbe Lowell, the congressman's newly hired lawyer. Within two hours, the meeting was set.

The attorneys booked a private dining room at the famous Jefferson Hotel, near the White House.

At the last minute Bob elected not to attend — he could not bear to be in the same room with Condit.

"I was too angry and I wanted to ask direct questions,

pointed questions," he admitted. "And when Condit and his lawyer set up the meeting, they didn't want those kind of questions."

Susan added softly, "My husband was too emotionally distraught. He was crying. He was really upset, and we just didn't think it would be good."

At the Jefferson Hotel, Susan sat next to Billy Martin on one side of a dining table; Condit and Lowell sat opposite them. Lowell was a recognizable and formidable hired gun, a man who had been all over television during President Clinton's impeachment hearings as lead attorney for the congressional Democrats. Condit would eventually employ a team of such legal spin masters for his defense.

Susan was offered tea, and the attorneys began talking. Susan could not wait to get to the four questions burning in her mind. Finally, it was her turn to speak. She looked Gary Condit directly in the eye.

"When's the last time you've seen my daughter — the date?"

"April 24," Condit replied.

"Where did you see my daughter?"

"In my house." Susan remembered that Condit spoke coldly.

"Your house in Ceres?"

"No, in my house in Washington, D.C."

"Do you happen to know where my daughter is?"

"No."

"Will you cooperate with our investigators and the police in the case?"

"Yes, I will cooperate fully. Mrs. Levy, I will do everything to help you find your daughter."

The meeting lasted no more than forty minutes, but Susan was emotionally drained. She had observed Gary

Condit's body language carefully throughout, and it told her, she claimed, that he was "hiding a whole lot."

As the meeting broke up, Condit held out his arms and asked Susan if he could give her a hug. She drew back from him abruptly and refused. Grimacing, she explained, "I couldn't stand the thought of him hugging me."

✳✳✳✳✳✳✳✳✳✳✳✳

After all their frustrations, the Levys were at least encouraged by a sudden switch in tactics by the FBI. The bureau moved the case up a few notches in importance by reassigning it to the D.C. field office's major case squad, established to handle difficult, long-term investigations.

The new agent in charge, Melissa Thomas, was a tough and successful veteran whose expertise was so well-known that she had been hired as a consultant on the Hollywood movie *Hannibal*, about a female FBI agent who hunted a serial killer. At Thomas's side on the Levy case was another FBI legend, agent Brad Garrett, who had a string of high-profile arrests under his belt.

In 1997, Garrett made headlines by leading the hunt and capture of a man who had eluded police for four years after killing two federal employees outside CIA headquarters in Virginia. Two years before that, he built the case that convicted the killer of three Starbucks coffee shop workers.

Thomas and Garrett had a squad of twelve agents working under them, and with that much muscle on the case, the Levys tried to tell themselves, they had to find Chandra now.

CHAPTER 13

Before Bob and Susan had left for Washington, D.C., a friend had suggested they take empty duffel bags so they could fill them with Chandra's belongings from her apartment.

Bob refused, because he felt it would be an admission that their daughter was never coming back to claim her things for herself.

While they were in Washington, Bob spent every conscious minute looking out the car windows, the police headquarters windows, the hotel windows, seeking his daughter's familiar face.

"I'm looking in the grass, in the trees," he said.

Back home in Modesto, every time the phone rang, Susan or Bob would fly to answer it, praying it was Chandra. Bob, frequently in tears, returned to work at the hospital after five weeks, but when he came home he spent evenings with his head buried in his wife's shoulder as they sat together on the sofa, watching for news flashes that might give some hope.

They made no secret of their pain. "It's just like a knife in our hearts that stops there and doesn't leave," said Bob hopelessly.

Susan took sleeping pills and tranquilizers and called frequently on God for the strength to go on. She also began sleeping in her daughter's room with the white wooden shades closed, because it made her feel closer to Chandra and somehow provided comfort.

Although they both desperately wanted to believe that Chandra was still alive, each was haunted by a dream in which she said goodbye.

"Susan had the first dream — and it was during a night when she slept in Chandra's bed," said a longtime family friend. "She told us she saw a very young Chandra dressed in her favorite Little League baseball uniform, waving goodbye to her.

"The very next night, Bob dreamed of Chandra in her high school graduation gown — and again she was waving farewell."

The parents were so disconcerted by their dreams that neither dared mention it to the other at first. Then one morning a week later, as they sat eating breakfast, Bob could hold back no longer. Susan was talking about Chandra when he interrupted her.

"I had this dream," he announced hurriedly. And with his voice quavering, he described what he had seen.

"Susan looked at him in horror, then broke down in tears," explained the friend. "Then she admitted that she had virtually the same dream."

The Levys left Chandra's bedroom exactly as it had been the day she had first departed for Washington in September 2000. It remained the bright and cheerful refuge of a young woman ready to step out into the world, the cherished retreat where she packed her bags and made farewell phone calls to friends in California.

The room's beige and white walls were covered with photos, awards, and diplomas. Her cosmetics case and a jewelry box stood on a gleaming white rattan dresser and a matching chest of drawers that reflected the brilliant morning sun. A crammed corner bookshelf held a dog-eared copy of *Men Are from Mars, Women Are from Venus*. A colorful wooden toucan, bought during an exotic vacation, gazed blindly out of the window, and a portable CD player sat on the floor beneath the window.

There were so many memories of Chandra's happy adolescence here. The Modesto police department emblems she collected when she was an Explorer Scout working with the local cops. San Francisco Giants souvenirs. And in a place of honor, the ticket stubs from the 1989 World Series game her father had taken her to.

To Bob and Susan, the ordinary possessions their daughter left behind were a heartbreaking yet comforting reminder of the young woman who had been so eager to take her first confident step out into the world.

"Now Bob can't bear to watch the Giants, because it reminds him so much of his daughter," said the family friend.

"And when Susan's pain is worst, she retreats to Chandra's room to look at photos like the one of their daughter lined up with her Little League team. Then she often meditates before she goes back to harsh reality."

Chandra's younger brother, Adam, also drew strength from the bedroom, working there on a model of the Eiffel Tower he was making with toothpicks.

Psychologist Jamie Turndorf, a specialist in relationships and family counseling, has seen recent photographs of the room and believes it betrays many of Chandra's closest secrets.

"When many young women leave home, they don't leave behind things like their jewelry boxes, clocks, cosmetics, or hair spray," said Turndorf. "But Chandra did — and it indicates that she had mixed feelings about growing up or separating from her parents. She had one foot in the adult world, but kept the other still planted firmly in her childhood.

"The mixed messages here are typical of a woman who could be lured into a liaison with a married man. The makeup and beauty products indicate she wanted to be attractive to men. But the prominent display of her diplomas and graduation tassel show career also was important to her. The fact that both types of items are equally visible indicates she was conflicted about where life was taking her.

"Chandra was still asking herself, 'Do I want to be a career woman? Or do I want to snag a boyfriend?'"

For Bob and Susan in their grief, none of those questions mattered. Their daughter's room was a sanctuary, a place where she was still with them.

Susan had known tragedy before — when she was sixteen her father killed himself as his business crashed. Although she somehow managed to deal with that, losing a child was far worse.

One day on the spur of the moment, Susan, who readily admits that she's a "little nutsy," signed up at Modesto Junior College for a vocal-jazz course.

Two *Washington Post* reporters, Richard Leiby and Petula Dvorak, tracked her down there and described the scene:

"Her voice is strained, she's hitting sour notes and botch-

Modeling dreams: One of 30 glamour shots taken by a commercial photographer when Chandra was a 17-year-old aspiring model. Her modeling career never took off, but this photo would be shown in newspapers around the world as police hunted for the missing intern.

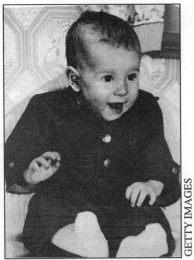

Chandra — cute as a button.

Chandra was a
freshman with braces
when she posed for
her 1992 Grace M.
Davis High School
yearbook photo.

Chandra's name in Sanskrit
means "daughter higher than
the moon and stars."

Teen Chandra
during a family
trip to Africa.

Chandra and her mom Susan, a sculptor.

The Levy family: Dad Bob, brother Adam and Chandra.

Chandra (center) was an intern with California Gov. Gray Davis, shown here with his wife Sharon.

Chandra and L.A. Mayor Richard Riordan are all smiles during her 3-month internship in his lobbying office.

Gary Condit, Chandra Levy and her friend Jennifer Baker — the girls' first visit to his Washington office.

Chandra rented a small apartment at the Newport in the upscale Dupont Circle neighborhood of D.C.

Chandra working at a laptop. Her Internet searches would later provide crucial clues to investigators.

MISSING

CHANDRA ANN LEVY

The Metropolitan Police Department is seeking the public's assistance in locating 24-year-old **Chandra Ann Levy**, who hasn't been seen in public since April 30th.

The Missing Person's notice posted by Washington police. The photo is from Chandra's teenage modeling shot.

Mister Blow Dry in 1978, on the
Stanislaus County Board of Supervisors.

Condit with son Chad, daughter Cadee and wife Carolyn
after winning a State Assembly seat in 1982.

Gary Condit in his leather chaps at a 1995
Christmas party in his Modesto office.

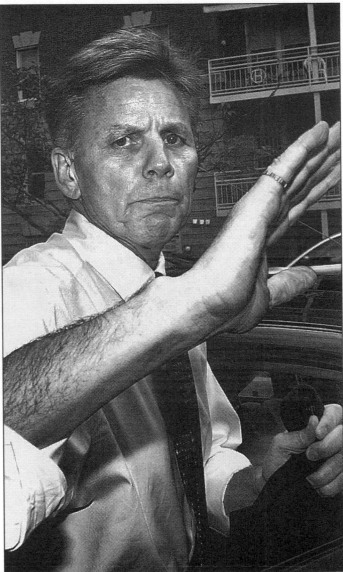

A harried Condit gestures toward a photog as he leaves
home on July 30, 2001, en route to his office.

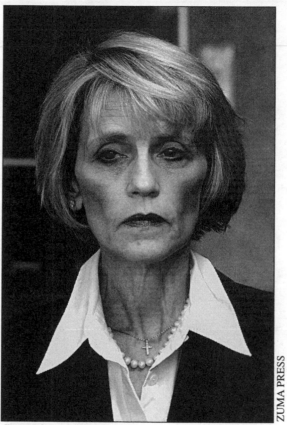

Stern-faced Carolyn Condit after the Chandra
scandal made headlines.

Condit is interviewed by Connie Chung on August 23, 2001. He refused to admit he had an affair with Chandra.

Susan Levy visits Chandra's room in her Modesto home, more than 10 weeks after the intern vanished.

Bob and Susan Levy, with their attorney Billy Martin, meet reporters in D.C. on June 21, 2001.

Gary Condit's top aide Mike Dayton fields questions about the congressman during an Aug. 30, 2001 interview.

Condit attorney Abbe Lowell makes another point to the press.

Condit galpals, L-R: Torrie Hendley, Anne Marie Smith and Joleen Argentini

PETER BRANDT

ZUMA PRESS

ZUMA PRESS

Gary Condit's brother Darrell has a long rap sheet dating back to 1968.

Aunt Linda Zamsky, Chandra's confidante, arrives at the Levy home the day after the intern's remains were found.

AP/WIDE WORLD PHOTO

A stake marks the spot where Chandra Levy's skull was found in Washington's Rock Creek Park.

Rock Creek's Klingle Mansion. Chandra searched the Internet for its location the day she disappeared.

Last photo: Chandra celebrates her 24th birthday — just weeks before she vanished. She's wearing the bracelet that was a gift from Gary Condit.

ing lyrics, but Susan Levy is determined to sing this song. 'All I need is one of your smiles — sunshine of your eyes,' she croons, accompanied by an indulgent jazz instructor and pianist. 'Give me lovin' — baby, I feel high.' Popular nearly forty years ago, the song just bubbled up like an intoxicating memory from her youth: *Scotch and Soda* by the Kingston Trio. It took her mind off her missing daughter, if only for a few moments.

"And that is why we find the mother of Chandra Levy standing at the front of a vocal-jazz classroom this afternoon ... singing, 'Oh me, oh my, do I feel high.'"

Afterwards, Susan tried to explain. Somehow she had to try to maintain a semblance of a normal life — otherwise she couldn't go on.

Still, when Bob and Susan were alone, they played the inescapable game "if only." If only Chandra had decided to be a doctor, as her father had wanted ... If only she had stayed at home instead of going to Washington ... If only they had never left Ohio ... If only.

CHAPTER 14

Gary Condit at first must have felt things were going to be all too easy. His initial interview with the police, held on May 15th, was little more than a chat. It took place not at police headquarters, but in the comforting surroundings of his condo, and he "somehow found a way to avoid answering one question — whether he and Chandra had been intimate," said a source familiar with the interview.

Moreover, Condit strangely neglected to mention to the detectives that his wife was visiting during the crucial days of Chandra's disappearance. Police learned that interesting news later from television. One of Condit's many lawyers, Joe Crotchett, let it slip while being interviewed on *Good Morning America*.

Yet Condit's expensive lead attorney, Abbe Lowell, managed to put an amazing spin on the first police interview.

"Congressman Condit tried to balance the need to cooperate with police while holding onto the privacy of his family and private life," he told reporters. "He didn't lie, and

[he] answered questions about every issue of significance, whether she was depressed, whether they went to specific restaurants, whether they traveled out of town, and where the police might look for Chandra Levy."

After hearing secondhand about Mrs. Condit's presence in town at the time of Chandra's disappearance, the police decided they needed to talk to Condit again. In mid-June they knocked on the door of his home in Adams Morgan without an invitation.

Condit would not speak with them, asserting, "It's not a good time."

A couple days later, on June 18th, the police visited his congressional office but found he was not in. When they returned on June 20th, Condit told them he was too busy to talk. *The New York Post* looked into his activities that day and found that he enjoyed a long two-and-a-half-hour lunch with a colleague and he also worked out in the congressional gym.

But Condit knew he couldn't stall forever, and on June 22nd he called the police and scheduled a second interview.

The following day, investigators finally talked to Condit again and, for the first time, were given an indication of the true relationship between him and Chandra. But the information was strictly off the record, they were made to understand.

Before the interview began, Lowell took the supervisory detective Jack Barrett aside and told him that for the purposes of the interview, the police could assume that Condit and Chandra had an intimate relationship.

"Lowell's motive was to avoid [Condit's] having [to make] a direct answer to an embarrassing question, an answer that Lowell was convinced would leak out to the press through one of the myriad of anonymous sources," explained Michael Doyle, the Washington correspondent for the *Modesto Bee*.

The proactive admission by the attorney worked perfectly, no doubt instantly earning Lowell his entire fee. Astonishingly, the police refrained from asking Condit the direct question of whether he and Chandra had been lovers, despite the fact that the affair could have been the crucial clue to cracking the case.

Still, Condit's luck couldn't last.

"As it happened, police ended up calling a third interview, in part so they could ask Condit the direct question," said Doyle.

The third interview took place on the evening of July 6th, a full sixty-seven days after Chandra's disappearance. When the question was finally put to Condit during the ninety-minute session, he conceded that he and Chandra had been much more than friends. They had been lovers, he admitted.

Just as Abbe Lowell had feared, within minutes after Condit left the interview, Internet news services and radio and TV stations were reporting his bombshell admission. Executive Assistant Police Chief Terrance Gainer told reporters that Condit had been "challenged" to clarify the relationship.

The truth was, that morning the *Washington Post* had printed Linda Zamsky's damning recollections of her "girl talks" with Chandra, and other sordid details of Condit's sexual escapades were beginning to surface in the media. Moreover, just the day before, Carolyn Condit had been interviewed for several hours by FBI agents in an office in northern Virginia.

Only after all this did Chief Ramsey declare of Condit's tardy admission that he'd been Chandra's lover, "It would have been very helpful if we had known that earlier on."

Maybe they should have asked earlier on.

Congressman Condit now had another major problem on his hands. There were flaws in his alibi for May 1st, the day Chandra vanished, and they raised troubling questions. He told police he had a private meeting with Vice President Dick Cheney that lasted from 12:30 to 1:15 p.m., fifteen minutes after Chandra logged off her computer for the last time. They discussed the California energy crisis and the vice president's energy plan.

Cheney's office was slow to confirm the meeting, apparently because aides were reluctant to let their boss be drawn into the scandal, but eventually, on July 20th, they did so.

In a timeline his office provided, Condit also claimed that he had a doctor's appointment between 5 and 6:30 p.m. He was later forced to trim that to between 5 and 5:30. What's more, said a source close to the case, "He says he went to a chiropractor, but, incredibly, at one point he told police he couldn't remember the doctor's name or address."

Condit's activities for the rest of that day are unclear. He said he was in and around his office in the afternoon and may have worked out at the House gym. And when his office first released the timeline, it showed an hour-long meeting at "a neighborhood coffee shop" — it turned out to be Tryst, the restaurant where he first had dinner with Chandra — with ABC-TV reporter Rebecca Cooper at 6:30 p.m., after his doctor's appointment.

The problem with that account was that Cooper quickly revealed it was wrong. She actually met Condit the following day, May 2nd. Condit then revised the schedule, saying he had in fact returned to the House, where he cast two votes on resolutions involving autism and supporting

National Charter Schools Week. He said he also submitted a prepared statement praising a retiring sheriff-coroner in his home district in California — a routine matter that is usually handled by a staff member, Capitol Hill experts quickly pointed out.

By about 7 p.m., Condit was back at his condo in Adams Morgan, where, he said, he ate dinner with his wife Carolyn and spent the rest of the evening.

munity that both families were a part of. He sorrowfully

When Chandra first arrived in Washington in the early fall 2001, the city was still buzzing with gossip about Monica Lewinsky, the twenty-one-year-old White House intern whose steamy sexual affair with President Clinton brought him to the brink of impeachment.

In pursuit of *her* forbidden man, Monica had reached even higher up the ladder of power than Chandra, brazenly enticing Bill Clinton in the White House itself with a flash of her thong underwear. And the nation had watched the revelations of the secret romance between Monica and Bill unfold with as much fascination as it now devoted to Chandra and Gary.

So the comparisons between Monica and Chandra were inevitable.

Nowhere were the parallels between the two cases so closely drawn as in a powerful sermon by the noted Rabbi Samuel M. Stahl, a respected member of the Jewish community that both families were a part of. He sorrowfully titled it "Chandra, Monica and American Jewry," but it blasted Gary Condit, too.

"Like Monica Lewinsky before her, Chandra Levy became another star in this ongoing Washington soap opera," the rabbi's words gripped the members of his temple from the opening sentence.

"Chandra had been a stereotypically good girl except for one problem — she had a weakness for married men. She had two or three affairs with other married men prior to her tryst with Gary Condit. Eventually she demanded that Condit leave his wife and enter into a permanent relationship with her. He obviously balked and rejected her."

The rabbi then thundered, "Condit himself is a paradoxical and hypocritical public figure. To his constituents, he tries to be a symbol of rectitude and conservatism. Though he is a Democrat, he has the most reactionary voting record of any Democrat in Congress.

"As we prepare for the High Holy Days we ponder the fact that Condit has indicated no remorse and no desire to confess and change, two primary steps in the repentancy process.

"There are other Jewish religious dimensions to this case," the rabbi continued. "The parallels between Monica and Chandra are striking. Both girls are Jewish. In fact Chandra's paternal grandparents survived the Holocaust. Chandra's favorite piece of jewelry is a necklace featuring the 'hand of God' that her parents bought her in Israel. Furthermore, the fathers of Monica and Chandra are oncologists. In their twenties, both girls became sexually active with married men who are three decades older and hold influential posts."

With his audience hanging on his every word, Rabbi Stahl ended his bombshell sermon with a lament.

"In some ways," he said, "Monica and Chandra are examples of the spiritual deterioration marring segments of the American Jewish Community. Monica and Chandra are daughters of wealthy Jewish parents. They grew up in affluent neighborhoods. Their parents are able to indulge their daughters' material needs, so that they can live comfortably in lovely quarters in a city where rents are steep.

"Both families seem to have lost their moral compass. Monica told her mother about her affair with Bill Clinton in the Oval Office, but her mother never said that she shouldn't behave like this. Chandra confided to her aunt about her ties with Condit. Instead of advising her to stay away from married men, her aunt gave her suggestions on how to win him.

"What about the embarrassment and shame that these two Jewish girls bring to all of us in the American Jewish Community?"

The rabbi didn't need to tell Susan Levy about embarrassment. She admitted that the public rumors seething around her daughter's sex life and her portrayal as a temptress were hard on her and the family.

"I'm embarrassed in a lot of ways, but Chandra is an adult," she said. "It's not like she was sixteen years old. She's twenty-four and a woman. She is not a slut, as some people have quoted in the news media, and I think she's very much in love with this particular person.

"Children want to spread their wings, and they're gifts of ours … but not ours. We taught our children morality, but you can teach a child what you think is correct — right and wrong — but still they make their choices."

She shook her head wearily. "If I didn't have my belief in God, what would I have?" she asked.

Susan, who said she's "old-fashioned" in her values,

recalled having a conversation about married men with her daughter while the two of them worked out together at a local gym.

"Chandra was saying, 'But what if the person is in a bad marriage?' Things like that."

The suffering mother closed her eyes and added, "You can't tell a kid what to do all the time."

****

On May 25th, more than a dozen police officers searched the woods near a popular jogging trail in Adams Morgan, looking for clues in the case of Chandra Levy's disappearance. Chief Ramsey was at pains to tell reporters that the proximity of the trail to Condit's apartment had no bearing on the search.

"It's just coincidence that he lives there and that he knows her," he said.

In mid-July, trained dogs were brought in to begin a door-to-door search of abandoned buildings near the Levy and Condit residences. The police picked their way gingerly through drug paraphernalia, but found nothing.

The FBI's Computer Analysis and Response Team examined Chandra's computer in early June, sending it to a lab where its hard drive was searched for deleted e-mails and files that might provide clues.

"People usually don't know how much information they're leaving behind," said expert Lawrence Rogers.

The lab reported that Chandra's laptop had proved to be a gold mine of information about her mental state in the hours before she vanished. It told detectives that whatever had happened, her obsession with Condit was all-consuming on the morning of May 1, 2001. Condit was literally the last person on Chandra's mind before she disappeared, the FBI agents discovered, uncovering the intern's three-hour Internet search for any article that mentioned the congressman.

From this police learned of Chandra's visit to MapQuest, the Web site that had provided her directions to the Klingle Mansion in Rock Creek Park. Yet, inexplicably, it wasn't until July 16th — nearly eleven weeks after Chandra was last seen — that fifty police recruits assembled in the park to begin scouring the vicinity of the mansion.

Television cameras followed the searchers as they walked in sweeping lines, tracing a grid pattern through the park and looking for anything that would indicate a body or a freshly dug grave. The images were beamed across the nation via satellite.

Watching the search on television at home, the Levys found themselves torn between wanting Chandra to be found and simultaneously not wanting her to be found.

"It's horrible, just painful to look at," said Susan, who admitted that deep in her heart she wanted the searchers to fail. On the other hand, it irritated her that the search seemed so nonchalant.

"They're not looking properly," she added.

The coverage was inevitably followed by footage of Gary Condit. The congressman was under siege. Half a dozen TV crews were camped outside his home twenty-four hours a day, and they waited on the doorstep every morning when he left the apartment to attend meetings. Reporters even lined the House hearing room.

Fellow congressmen on the Agriculture Committee, on which Condit was the second-ranking Democrat, joked that it was the first time they had ever seen TV cameras recording what were usually the driest of hearings.

No one watched Condit's daily comings and goings on television more intently than Bob and Susan Levy, 3,000 miles away in Modesto. They came to hate the frozen grin he invariably wore for the cameras.

"I see a man going from his congressional meetings with his fake political smile, and the physical action does not match a person who says they really want to help you out," said Susan bitterly.

The search by the police in Rock Creek Park around the Klingle Mansion ended after two fruitless weeks. The recruits needed to return to classes at the academy, said Chief Ramsey, and they had found little more than animal bones and trash.

Ten months later, he would have to admit that they had probably walked within 100 yards of Chandra's body.

CHAPTER 16

While the circumstances of Chandra's disappearance remained murky, the world heard sordid tales of a secret life led by Condit, churned out by the notorious Washington rumor mill cranking up to full steam.

Former U.S. Congressman John LeBoutillier, now an Internet columnist, wrote in a July 13, 2001, article that Condit, a motorcycle buff, frequently engaged in gay sex with bikers who visited his Washington, D.C., neighborhood.

"Here's the dirty little secret behind the disappearance of Chandra Levy: Condit goes both ways," LeBoutillier freely claimed. "The gay sex turns him on so he can then 'perform' with women."

LeBoutillier even theorized that Condit ordered one of his regular Caribbean male partners to take care of Chandra, because she was about to spill the beans on her lover's kinky habits.

Police officers looking for Chandra inevitably heard

those rumors and found themselves probing the seedy side of Washington's gay community. One of their targets was a thirty-six-year-old computer Web designer known as Washington's most notorious S&M dungeon master. Inside his apartment, the computer whiz trained gay men in acts of bondage, flogging, and simulated torture. He then posted pictures of his submissive followers on an elaborate Internet site.

Reportedly, the dungeon master bragged to others that he had taught a congressman and his girlfriend all of his special techniques.

One of his many admitted slaves claimed that those two people were Gary Condit and Chandra Levy.

Already in shock, Bob and Susan Levy heard that FBI agents were indeed probing allegations of kinky ménage à trois sex sessions involving Chandra, Condit, and a male lover.

If that image didn't give the Levys nightmares, another theory about Chandra's disappearance certainly haunted their days and nights — was Chandra kidnapped and tortured to death by foreign assassins?

As cloak-and-dagger as it sounds, the possibility was taken seriously. Condit was a veteran of the House Select Committee on Intelligence, whose members have access to America's most vital security secrets. Suddenly a man who knew everything about the secret operations of our nation's spymasters was at the center of a missing-person case involving his young mistress, and it did not go unnoticed.

FBI agents, CIA officials, investigators for the House of Representatives, and even Interpol all had the same question: What if Condit, in pillow talk with his lover, let slip some of the nation's secrets?

"This guy is made-to-order for blackmail," said former

CIA officer Duane "Dewey" Claridge, citing Condit as a potential security risk nightmare. The love affair also made Chandra a prime kidnapping target for America's enemies if Condit had shared any top-secret information with her.

"If terrorists found out Chandra knew anything about Condit's work on the Intelligence Committee, she'd be kidnapped, tortured for information, and killed," said one House investigator, putting words to the fears intimated by intelligence agencies.

Former Congressman Robert Dornan urged the House leadership to remove Condit from the Intelligence Committee. His loose morals, said Dornan, left him open to "all sorts of pressure from foreign interests not friendly to the U.S."

As the days passed and Chandra remained missing, investigators went so far as to look at links between Condit and Arab oil dealers involved with the human slave trade in the Middle East.

"Condit got to know these shady oilmen because he enjoys the company of Middle Eastern women," a source on the D.C. police force revealed. Condit, said the source, was known to frequent the bars at Washington's poshest hotels, where the oil bigwigs and their Middle Eastern girlfriends gathered.

Author and *Vanity Fair* sleuth Dominick Dunne also threw a Middle Eastern connection into the mix of theories about Chandra's whereabouts. Dunne claimed to have "uncovered new leads" that showed the missing intern may have stumbled into a ring of prostitution, sex slaves, and Middle Eastern sheiks that might have contributed to her disappearance. Dunne said the leads came from a reliable informant who was a well-known procurer of women for Middle Eastern diplomats in Washington.

The informant, said Dunne, revealed that in the weeks after Chandra vanished, he had met an impeccably dressed, well-connected Middle Eastern man who claimed to have seen the intern being carried onto a private jet surrounded by five men. Chandra either had been dumped over the Atlantic or was in a harem in the Middle East.

Dunne, who passed the lead on to the FBI, later traveled to England where a meeting with the informant had been prearranged.

The man never showed.

Two private investigators hired by the Levy family, Joe McCann and Dwayne Stanton, former homicide detectives on the D.C. police force, described other amazingly remote theories regarding Chandra's disappearance. Phone tips to a family hotline produced one bizarre lead after another.

At times the hotline seemed like Psychic Central as calls poured in from clairvoyants who could "see" the exact location of Chandra's body.

One said he was positive Chandra's body rested in a small body of water near D.C.

"He paid the drainage costs," recalled McCann. "The body wasn't there."

Psychic Ariel Love, whose paranormal abilities have been recognized by researchers at Duke University, knew a friend of Susan Levy and offered her help. Feeling she had nothing to lose, Susan called Love. The psychic said she wanted some of Chandra's personal items to hold. Susan provided a candle, a makeup case, and a baseball cap.

Love's conclusion was grisly.

"When Chandra left her apartment for the last time that fateful day, she had dreams of living happily every after," Love said.

"I really hope I'm wrong, but the energy I'm getting is

very strong and only points in one direction — Chandra's murder."

So-called remote-viewers also chimed in with offers to use the special gifts they claimed to have. Remote-viewers contend they have the ability to experience, feel, see, and describe detailed information on any event, person, being, place, process, or object that has ever existed, does exist, or will exist.

A remote-viewer group called PSI, which boasts the motto "Mind is the final frontier," put their final frontiers together and came to these conclusions about Chandra:

"She is dead. The body location is in a dark, gloomy desolate terrain, near a passageway, where foghorns or train horns and birds are the main silence breakers. There are indicators that Chandra was in the early stage of pregnancy. She died by asphyxiation. The murderer was a young Caucasian man in his 20s with very short hair. Chandra's death was a deliberate act."

Another tipster suggested that Chandra's disappearance might be linked to the suicide of a top agricultural labor official, David Moore, who was a crony of Condit's. Moore was head of the powerful Western Growers Association, an influential lobbying group whose members grow, pack, and ship ninety percent of the fresh vegetables and seventy percent of the fresh fruit and nuts in California and Arizona.

On June 6, 2001, at age sixty-nine, Moore shot himself in his Irvine, California, office with a .45 Colt revolver. A press release put out by the Growers Association said that he was survived by his remarkable wife of forty-nine years, Priscilla, and that he had eleven grandchildren to whom "he was the most fun Papa ever." The obituary did not mention the suicide.

After commenting that Moore was in general "a happy

fellow," the tipster suggested that there was a more sinister motive for his suicide, some secret information about Chandra and Condit that was eating him up inside.

As a member of the House Agricultural Committee, Condit knew Moore well. The congressman had thrown his clout enthusiastically behind the Western Growers Association and other groups to back a California water bond issue favorable to farmers. Provoking the anger of environmentalists, Condit used his political weight to support measures backed by Moore's group that would have delayed the banning of the deadly ozone-depleting pesticide methyl bromide.

Look for a link between Condit and Moore's suicide, the tipster urged.

A review of Moore's long, detailed suicide note quickly laid all of this to rest. The man had been tortured by many things — none of which related to Chandra Levy or Gary Condit.

From all around the country, Chandra sightings were also being reported to police officials and the Levy investigators. Chandra look-alikes were showing up everywhere.

While shopping in a Home Depot, a woman who resembles the missing intern suddenly found herself being asked, "Hey, aren't you Chandra Levy?"

"Actually, it was sort of a compliment," the woman said. "She's twenty-two years younger than me."

Don Seger, an eighty-year-old retiree from Phoenix, was so sure he had spotted the missing intern that he placed repeated calls to the FBI until he finally got an agent to take his information. He also rang up the Levy family, left a message, and got a call back from Bob, who listened to Seger's tale.

Seger had been on a road trip with his wife, Betty, when

the two of them stopped for a bite to eat at the cafeteria of the famed Mayo Clinic in Scottsdale, Arizona. A young woman seated at a nearby table caught his eye. She looked very familiar and then it hit him — it's Chandra Levy — that missing intern whose picture had been plastered all over the TV news.

"I wasn't the only person looking at her. There were others in the cafeteria who were staring at her too," said Seger.

The woman looked pregnant.

"She had an Indian blanket wrapped around her lower half, which seemed funny because it was something like 110 degrees. It was like she was using the blanket to hide her pregnancy. She was holding an envelope and there was an elderly woman with her, who was dressed in a uniform, like she worked for the clinic.

"At one point, the young lady got up and went to get a glass of water and a straw. When she came back to the table, she crossed her legs and I saw a small tattoo above her left ankle that looked like a little flower about the size of a silver dollar.

"Dr. Levy told me about the rose tattoo Chandra had, that it had a little stem on it. He seemed real thrilled about my information. There was almost a relief in his voice."

But relief was always followed by near despair for the tortured father as the next tip about the location of Chandra's body came in.

The Levy's private investigators spent weeks exploring an incredibly detailed story of Chandra's death during a botched abortion. The yarn came from a gun-toting loner in his mid-sixties named Pat Russ, whose home was a shack in Stockton, California.

Russ is a convicted arsonist, who, by his own admission, has set about two thousand fires across the country for personal as well as professional reasons. The worst was a 1971 blaze that destroyed 16,100 acres in Santa Barbara's Los Padres National Forest. Four men were killed in the fire. Russ said he started the inferno after his wife left him for another man — his brother.

"I felt I'd been dealt a losing hand and somebody was gonna pay," he said, trying to justify his insanity, which was the plea that sent him to Atascadero State Hospital for four years. After he was released, Russ became the star of a series of firefighter training films titled "An Arsonist Talks."

He was in a talking mood when investigators McCann and Stanton showed up at his Stockton shack to hear his story about Chandra.

Russ said that he had received an interesting phone call from an old friend in mid to late April, just before Chandra disappeared. The friend, whom Russ described as "a very connected Washington man," was acting on the instructions of Gary Condit and needed a favor from the firebug.

As McCann and Stanton took notes, Russ explained that he was asked to drive a Winnebago from Stockton to Denver on May 2nd, the day after Chandra disappeared. This he did, arriving near midnight at the prearranged meeting spot, the parking lot of a Denny's restaurant. Two men, whose names had been given to Russ, were waiting with Chandra Levy, who was obviously in a drugged-out state. The arsonist described one of the men as a doctor with a shady past.

"When you get a bullet in the leg and you want to keep it hush-hush, he's the guy you go to," said Russ.

After packing a wobbly Chandra into the Winnebago, the three men got into the vehicle, and her guardians told Russ to make a beeline for Reno, Nevada. It was a sixteen-hour drive, and Chandra was heavily medicated the entire way.

"She slept most of the way but occasionally woke up and spoke in blurry tones," Russ told the Levy investigators.

"She was wearing a pink top and blue pants and sandals with no socks. She had a tattoo on her ankle in the shape of a flower. She was wearing a ring that had initials on it."

During the drive, Russ overheard the two men he was transporting talking about a female veterinarian based in Sparks, Nevada. This veterinarian was going to be the one to perform an abortion on Chandra.

After delivering his passengers to Reno, Russ was dismissed and headed back to Stockton. A few weeks later, he contacted the man who had initially hired him, and learned Chandra's fate.

The abortion had gone terribly wrong.

"She bled and she died," said Russ.

From what he garnered, Condit had set the whole thing up, essentially to get rid of his love child, and the death was an added bonus. Russ said he'd been told Chandra was becoming too demanding of the congressman, putting a lot of pressure on him to leave his wife. She was even criticizing legislation he was backing.

"She was getting too big for her britches," Russ added.

He predicted that no one would ever find Chandra's body.

"It's probably in pieces, strewn from one state to another," he told McCann and Stanton.

As incredulous as the story sounded, it had to be checked out. The names he mentioned were real people, the investigators learned.

"We know who the veterinarian is and she does have a ranch near Sparks," said McCann.

The two veteran investigators had also been around

long enough to know stranger things were a possibility.

It took the gumshoes weeks of digging before they finally were able to discount the arsonist's tale. As further details of the story proved incorrect, they employed the voice stress analyst Al Starewich to listen to an audiotape of Russ they had made. His verdict: Russ was lying.

The hope was that somewhere among all the rumors and dead ends that investigators inevitably have to go through was something of use. One such tip about Condit proved to have truth to it — and it only added to the Levys' fears that the congressman had something to do with their daughter's disappearance.

In the mid-1980s, there was talk in his California congressional district that two local teenage girls claimed Condit, who was then a state assemblyman, had sexually assaulted them.

The girls fled to Alaska, and *The National Enquirer* tracked down a former investigator who handled the case for the Alaska Crime Commission, a private organization dedicated to helping teens in trouble. The woman remembered the girls well.

"One said she was raped, the other that she was sexually assaulted . . . They were afraid Gary Condit was going to kill them. They'd been interns with him in his California office. They lived with their families in Modesto, his seat of power. I had a written statement from the two girls."

The girls were ultimately sent to live with relatives in Seattle, and no action was ever taken, the woman recalled. Mysteriously, their statements vanished in a burglary of the warehouse where they were stored.

The investigator, in explaining why she refused to be identified, said, "I'm in fear of my life — Condit is a dangerous man."

CHAPTER 17

Early in the evening on July 10, 2001, a man approached a trash can in a park in Alexandria, Virginia, and after glancing around quickly, tossed something into it. A random passerby thought the individual appeared familiar. Then he realized it was the same man all over the news of late, Gary Condit.

A phone call brought police to the location. They dug through the garbage, retrieving an empty french fry carton. Inside it was a box that had once contained a watch — a costly Tag Heuer. The box was engraved with a serial number that led investigators to the person who had bought the watch, Joleen Argentini, a former staff member in the offices of Congressman Gary Condit.

Police were already familiar with Joleen Argentini. Originally from Modesto, but now married and living in San Francisco, she had come forward a month earlier to detail her affair with the congressman in an effort to aid the search for Chandra Levy. Her story sounded eerily similar to that of the missing intern. They were both young and impressionable, drawn to the powerful congressman.

Joleen was only twenty-two when she was introduced to Condit at a dinner in Washington in 1992. At the time, she was dating the congressman's aide, Mike Dayton, who would prove to have no problem sharing girlfriends with his boss. Condit was instantly attracted to the beautiful young woman.

In October 1993, while living in Los Angeles, Joleen received an appealing invitation from Dayton to attend a Democratic fund-raiser featuring an appearance by President Bill Clinton. When she arrived at the hotel where Dayton was supposedly staying, however, only Condit met her there.

The two of them would be dining by themselves, the congressman announced, and the affair began.

In January 1994, Condit persuaded Joleen to move to Washington and work in his office as a $24,000-a-year staff assistant. To make things more convenient, he even gave her an airline ticket to D.C. Joleen soon rented a $700-a-month, two-bedroom basement flat, which she shared with a roommate. The apartment, located at 1918 Biltmore Street NW, was a two-minute walk from the congressman's condo.

"What a convenient love nest," said Frank Miele, the owner of the building, recalling the apartment. "Joleen's roommate was gone during the day so they would have had the place to themselves."

Besides working for Condit, Joleen secured a job at the City Fitness Gym in Washington, teaching an aerobics class. Her primary interest, however, was the congressman, who often brought her on double dates with other politicians and their mistresses.

A friend recalled that Joleen had confided to her that

she was romantically involved with a married man.

"She was genuinely in love with him — and she told me excitedly that he'd promised he was going to leave his wife and marry her," the friend said.

"One day she showed me an expensive gift she'd bought for him — a Tag Heuer watch in a fancy box."

Joleen had described to the friend certain "rules" that governed her affair with Condit. When the congressman wanted to see her, he would leave nonverbal messages on her answering machine, punching in a toned code.

Living this way "was so overwhelming to her" that Joleen began having sudden emotional outbursts in the congressman's Rayburn House Office Building headquarters, according to a co-worker.

During one office flare-up, Joleen revealed the depths her frustration and loneliness were reaching as her obsession with Condit intensified.

"I can't have any friends. He gets jealous," she blurted out to the co-worker. "He's very jealous."

On more than one occasion, Joleen barged into Condit's office, closed the door, and after a loud shouting match, emerged in tears. After one outburst more than he could take, Condit informed Joleen he was cutting her out of his life.

She immediately quit her job.

"She'd totally lost it," the friend explained. "We sat down and when I managed to stop her crying, she said she was going to have to go back to California. The congressman had broken up with her.

"He told her, 'It's all over' — and she was in utter depression. She was totally in love with this man and he destroyed her."

Condit wasn't finished with Joleen, however.

After moving to San Francisco, Joleen received a call from Condit in late 1994, and their relationship resumed.

"Gary always referred to Joleen as Peanut, a cute little nickname he made up for her," divulged Vince Flammini, Condit's former driver and bodyguard. "Of all the women he was juggling, Peanut was by far his favorite.

"Joleen lived in a pad off California Street, and Gary would have me drive him there — sometimes as often as several times a week," Flammini revealed. "Gary told me to park the car across the street and stay there until he got back. Sometimes he returned within an hour or two, and other times he stayed with her all night. Many times I was ordered to drop him off Friday night and pick him up on Sunday."

Joleen's hopes of becoming Mrs. Gary Condit, however, were short lived and never meant to be.

"Their final split was ugly," added Flammini.

"One night I drove Gary to Peanut's apartment and was told to wait outside. They had a huge argument and he stormed out of the building to my car. He immediately broke off the relationship. Peanut was so upset that she kept all of his clothes that were in her apartment — including a $400 Harley-Davidson leather jacket."

On May 16, 2001, sixteen days after Chandra vanished and a week after Condit sat down for his first interview with police, Joleen summoned up her courage and walked into the FBI offices in San Francisco. She told the agents about her affair with Condit, emphasizing that he required total loyalty and absolute secrecy and imposed rules to ensure this, just as he'd done with Chandra.

Joleen, recognizing how fortunate she was to have escaped Condit, contacted D.C. police to urge them to go over every inch of Chandra's apartment. She even made four phone calls to Mike Dayton, still Condit's aide, telling him the congressman should cooperate fully with authorities.

Joleen did not expect the answer she received from Dayton.

She was told to leave the affair she had with Condit "in the past, or it will ruin you." As for talking to authorities, Dayton allegedly added, "You don't want to do that." Dayton denies the comments.

Now investigators wondered why Condit was going to such lengths to dispose of a watch box. And why was he dumping it in a park miles from his condo? He may have just been trying to hide another marital infidelity. Or did the watch have something to do with Chandra's disappearance?

Speculation arose that Condit may have given the watch to Chandra.

"The watch case has the serial number of the watch on it," said an investigative source. "If Chandra's body is found and she's wearing the watch, Condit's actions are those of a man who doesn't want the case in his possession."

Mark Fuhrman, formerly a detective and now a crime commentator and author, called the watch "a very crucial, pivotal part of the investigation. Where is the watch? I'd be very much interested. Condit hasn't produced it."

Crime expert Robert Ressler, a former top FBI profiler, agreed that the watch box incident had guilt written all over it.

"Condit threw the box away because he felt it would open up doors," said Ressler. His actions speak of "paranoia . . . culpability or involvement."

Even more incriminating was the timing of Condit's trip

to the Alexandria trash can. Just hours later, at 11:30 p.m., Condit was back in his D.C. condo as six police lab technicians and a detective descended on the premises.

Condit, after a long negotiation with authorities, had finally given his permission for the search. After all, he claimed to have nothing to hide.

Or did he?

Until 3 a.m., the cops used ultraviolet lights, the blood-detecting chemical luminol, and other equipment to look for "blood, hair, telltale signs of a struggle" and other evidence of a crime, said D.C. Executive Assistant Police Chief Terry Gainer.

As Condit and his lawyer, Abbe Lowell, stood by, the investigators scoured every nook and cranny of the one-bedroom apartment, vacuuming particles from its two bathrooms and even using microscope equipment to scan its high ceilings. If there were clues, they intended to find them.

One thing the technicians noticed but didn't bring up during the search was the absence of a computer. It seemed odd to them in an Internet-crazy world. If Condit did have a computer, it was now long gone.

At one point, the technicians shined an ultraviolet light on venetian blinds in the apartment. A section of the blinds was subsequently cut and taken as evidence.

What the cops found raised even more questions: Semen stains were scattered throughout Condit's condo in more than a dozen locations.

"At first, detectives assumed that the samples were all from Condit," said a source close to the investigation, but tests revealed samples from "several different males." Was there truth to the charges that Condit was gay?

Or was he the host of orgies?

Aside from the semen stains, visible only with the lab technicians' high-tech toys, Condit's apartment afforded few clues.

Following the search, a law enforcement source told the *Washington Times* that the technicians remarked on "the cleanliness of the residence. It had been cleaned all over and was pretty neat."

Was getting rid of the watch box part of that "all over" cleaning? As suspicions grew about Condit's garbage-dumping trip to the Alexandria park, his supporters tried to pass off the incident as meaningless.

Mike Dayton, who reportedly drove his boss to the park and waited while Condit went to the trash can, said, "There's been a lot of hay made about that watch box, and I regret that it has added to suspicion. I sat down with police over a two-day period. I've told them everything I know about that."

Condit's daughter, Cadee, nearly laughed when she told CNN's Larry King, "The only thing I can say with the watch box is there were french fries involved."

Her smile fading, she added that the case of the missing intern had indeed brought on a profound change in her father.

"You know, I don't know if we'll ever get the twinkle back."

CHAPTER 18

Congressman Gary Condit was finally feeling the intense heat from his many affairs. It would soon boil over. A little black book full of former Condit conquests came forward to paint a disturbing portrait of the philandering politician with the confident smile and the blow-dried hair, each providing another crucial glimpse into the Casanova congressman's true dark character.

****

On May 17th, the day after Joleen talked to the FBI in San Francisco, a plane that had taken off in that city arrived in Washington, D.C. On board was a curvy California redhead, flight attendant Anne Marie Smith. Anne Marie had not yet heard of Chandra Levy's disappearance, having been too caught up with her very busy new job with United Air Lines.

That would be changing shortly.

Anne Marie's relationship with Congressman Condit was

approaching its first anniversary. Condit had been a passenger on board one of her flights from Washington to San Francisco in July 2000. Although he wasn't wearing a wedding ring, Condit told Anne Marie he was married but things were not good at home. He told her that Mrs. Condit was seriously ill with "encephalitis of the brain." Then he slipped Anne Marie one of his fancy cards with the congressional seal and the number for his private phone line.

She called soon after.

At thirty-nine years old, Anne Marie was fifteen years older than Chandra and, unlike the missing intern, did not have illusions that Condit was going to leave his wife for her. Her sexual get-togethers with the congressman included romps at hotels like the Hyatt near San Francisco Airport or, if she was in D.C., at Condit's condo.

On this trip, Anne Marie expected to hook up again with the congressman, but she soon realized something strange was going on. Six days earlier, on May 11th, she had received a disturbing phone message from Condit.

"I may be in trouble . . . I may have to disappear for a while . . . Don't call me for a few days, I'll call you . . . Or if you do call me, don't identify yourself and leave a very short message . . . Don't tell anyone about this phone call and don't talk to anybody about me if you hear my name."

Demonstrating his desire to maintain his old ways despite the current distractions and hopefully manage another rendezvous, Condit added confidently, "Everything is OK with you and me."

She turned on the television in her hotel room and in minutes knew what was up. The Chandra Levy case was all over the news, complete with details of how the missing intern had been linked romantically to Condit. The reports maintained that Condit was supposedly a happily married man, which was not the way he had described things to Anne Marie.

"I turned on the television and I heard the news," she said. "I called Gary and left him a message. And I was like, you need to explain this to me."

Anne Marie was pained to learn Condit had another lover, but that pain soon turned to fear.

A month before Chandra disappeared, Condit had started trying to take their relationship to kinkier heights that she felt were dangerous. Initially she thought he was joking when he said he would like to see her have sex with multiple lovers. Now she was rethinking everything in a new light.

"I felt very frightened," she admitted.

Condit called Anne Marie at her hotel room that night around midnight. Cops later learned that for some reason that was never explained, he was 80 miles away from D.C., using a pay phone outside a shuttered McDonald's in Luray, Virginia, an area known for its remote natural caverns.

According to Anne Marie, "Mr. Condit called me from Luray on my cell phone, saying, 'There is no way I can talk with you . . . Everything is OK between us.'"

She asked Condit if he was having an affair with Chandra Levy and if he had anything to do with her disappearance.

"I can't believe you're asking me these types of questions," Condit said, failing to deny either of them. "I'm just dealing with the situation." If Anne Marie thought he was guilty, Condit said, she would find out "she was dealing with the wrong man."

The flight attendant was so unnerved and uncertain of what Condit might be capable of that she called her sister and a girlfriend, assuring them she was not suicidal. She urged them to call the authorities if she suddenly vanished.

Anne Marie, recognizing the inevitable, then decided it was best if she told the FBI about her affair with the congressman. She went to see them on June 1, 2001, and found that the agents, having done their homework, already knew about her.

Talking for hours, Anne Marie provided intimate details of the way Condit handled his extracurricular activities. Once again the details revealed a developing pattern. He rarely took her out, and if he did, it would be to secluded tables in dimly lit bars or restaurants. She could never call him directly. Rather, she had to use a special number and leave a voicemail message — only then would he call back.

"When we were together in his D.C. condo, we would have to leave at a different time and I was told by Mr. Condit not to talk to his neighbors," Anne Marie admitted to the agents. "When we were on the street, Mr. Condit would wear a baseball hat and dark glasses. On several occasions, he would pretend not to know me, sometimes directing me ahead and then catching up with me."

Wanting to be up front with Condit, whom she still had feeling towards, Anne Marie called him and told him she had talked to the FBI that day.

"He was extremely angry," she explained. "He said that I didn't know what they were trying to do to him."

By the start of the second week of June, the flight attendant was still behind the scenes in the Chandra Levy case. But two of Anne Marie's friends, concerned about her emotional well-being, gave details of her affair with Condit to *Star* magazine, although Anne Marie's name was not published.

On June 13th, Anne Marie received a phone call from Mike Lynch, Condit's chief of staff, who instructed her to call the law firm of the congressman's California attorney, Joseph W. Cotchett. After doing so, she was directed to an individual named Don Thornton, who proceeded to ask question after question about what she had actually revealed to the federal investigators. Anne Marie cut off the conversation and contacted her own lawyer, James Robinson.

Robinson called Thornton and made it clear that all further contact with Anne Marie should be made through him.

He didn't have long to wait.

On June 15th, Robinson called Anne Marie to say he had received an affidavit from Thornton. Anne Marie was being asked to sign the document as soon as possible. It stated, in paragraph five, "I do not and have not had a romantic relationship with Congressman Gary Condit."

Robinson called Thornton and said, "Paragraph five is a complete and total lie."

After a pause, Thornton, according to Robinson, replied, "Can't you play with the language?"

"No," Robinson snapped, then called Anne Marie to explain she could go to jail for perjury if she signed such a document. The flight attendant realized that whatever affection Condit had for her was clearly history.

On June 29th, Robinson received a telephone call from Condit's Washington attorney, Abbe Lowell, who said he was "deeply concerned" that lawyer-client privilege did not protect recent conversations Anne Marie had been having with Condit.

Robinson, concerned and confused, checked with his client. Anne Marie, he learned, had been talking to Condit. But she said it was the congressman who'd been calling her, not the other way around. He was urging her to sign the affidavit.

"There were at least three or four phone calls from Mr. Condit," said Anne Marie. "He called me directly from Mr. Cotchett's office, saying it was a safe phone. He was saying, 'Well, I don't understand why your attorney will not let you sign it.' I knew I could never sign the document."

As the month of July began, Robinson admitted to having "grave concerns for Ms. Smith's safety," and he moved her from San Francisco to his hometown of Seattle.

At Robinson's urging, Anne Marie went public "as a way to protect herself." She was soon appearing on Fox News, the Larry King show, and *Good Morning America*, talking to Diane Sawyer and revealing a laundry list of Condit's secrets.

According to Anne Marie, Condit was beyond perverted. He liked to have phone sex with the flight attendant. He liked to use "toys" to heighten pleasure. Occasionally Condit wore full leather outfits during sex. He even urged her to take part in orgies with other male partners.

Said Robinson, "He told Anne Marie, 'I have a fantasy about a bunch of guys and one woman — you.'" One night at Condit's D.C. condo, Anne Marie had noticed "neckties tied together that were tied to the feet of the bed. They looked like they'd been there awhile."

When she asked him about the ties, Condit replied, "Oh, honey, I was thinking of doing that to you."

Robinson added Anne Marie realized that Condit was probably cheating on her when she found a strand of long black curly hair in his bathroom. Later, she concluded it was probably Chandra's.

CHAPTER 19

Torrie Hendley, a hazel-eyed brunette who worked as a Hollywood Studios driver, was at the Love Run biker weekend in Laughlin, Nevada, in April 1996 when she met the smooth-talking congressman.

As Torrie recalled that fateful day, she was setting up a stand to sell T-shirts that were decorated with her silkscreen artwork when a few boxes fell out of her truck and a handsome man came over to help.

A six-month affair began.

"He looked cute in his gray Harley T-shirt, black Levis, black biker boots and black leather jacket. It was obvious he worked out. He looked real good," Torrie explained. "He introduced himself as Gary Condit. His name didn't mean anything to me then. He bought a T-shirt and was very friendly. I liked him right away."

Torrie said Condit had biked to the event with a body-guard. The congressman asked her to hop on board his Harley and take a ride with him. "He wasn't wearing a wedding ring. I asked his bodyguard, 'Is this guy safe?'

The guy said, 'Gary's a very powerful man. You couldn't be more safe.'"

She went off with Condit for a ride in the desert. Later, Torrie and her friend Maureen were invited to hook up with their new friends at the bar of the Laughlin hotel, where the congressman was staying.

"He didn't smoke or drink," said Torrie.

"After a while, he asked me to come to his room. We sat down on the bed and started kissing and while we were kissing, he told me he wanted to sleep with me and I said, 'No way. I don't even know you.' That really shocked him. It was obvious he wasn't used to being turned down."

Torrie left Condit's room at 3 a.m., after giving him her home number in Burbank, California. Nearly every day for the next few weeks, Condit barraged Torrie with phone call after phone call.

Finally, he invited her to Washington, D.C., for the 1996 Memorial Day weekend.

"He flew me to D.C. on a red-eye flight — that's the very cheapest and all he'd actually pay for."

At the airport, Condit picked Torrie up in a beat-up old red Ford Escort.

"I joked with him about it. I said, 'What's a big shot like you doing driving a piece of shit like this?'" Condit blew up, revealing a hair-trigger temper that Torrie saw on more than one occasion.

"He got really mad and started shouting at me, calling me 'Miss Hollywood' and saying, 'You think image is so important. I make more money than you could ever make, but I don't have to show it.'"

Condit drove the woman to an apartment in a high-rise building and got down to business.

"I had hardly put my bags down when he started kissing

me and taking off my clothes. Pretty soon we were having sex on the couch. I asked him about condoms and he said he didn't like to wear them. He claimed he'd had a vasectomy and didn't have AIDS. And strangely, he said there was a cure for AIDS, anyway.

"He took off his shoes and jeans, but not his shirt or socks. He was so eager to have sex, there was no foreplay. I noticed every time afterward, he kept his socks on when we had sex."

During their escapades, Torrie said Condit had to be in control.

"He liked to be dominant," she explained. "He always wanted to be on top, pinning my arms down with his hands. He couldn't handle me being on top."

After that first apartment encounter, Condit moved Torrie to a suite at a convenient hotel in D.C. Then he disappeared for the rest of the day, not returning until the following morning.

"We went out for coffee, then came back to the room and had sex on the couch. He preferred having a quickie on the couch to using the bed. I think he got some kind of kinky kick out of it."

Condit's behavior grew stranger, said Torrie.

"He lay me across his lap and spanked me on my bare butt, but it just made me laugh, and that ticked him off. He said, 'What are you laughing at?' He didn't like to be made fun of."

The next night Condit was back. This time he brought a camera and tried to take pictures of Torrie undressing. Not wanting to be photographed, she satisfied another of his cravings.

"I let him chase me around the suite. When he caught me, he started kissing me and pulled off my nightie."

As their affair continued, Condit became fanatical about secrecy.

"He insisted we use code names. He said, 'You can be Millie and I'll be Floyd.' After that, he'd call me on the phone and say, 'Hi, Millie, what are you doing?' And I'd call him and say, 'Hey Floyd, what's up.'"

During their affair, Torrie said Condit flew her to Washington several times for sex sessions. "He would leave me in the morning at some hotel with $50 for walking around and taxi money and not return until evening. Then he'd come back, we'd eat and have sex."

Several times, Condit flew into Los Angeles for a little taste of Torrie, and it was during one of these visits that his hair-trigger temper flared up again.

She was supposed to have met Condit at the Airport Hilton at 7:30 p.m., but she had drunk too much at a friend's bachelorette party. She didn't arrive until midnight.

"He was furious. He yelled, 'I have got better things to do than wait around for you all night.'" They went to get something to eat but the hotel restaurant was already closed. "When we got back to the room, he turned on the TV and refused to talk to me. He sat there pouting. I laughed and tried to tickle him and muss his hair, which made him madder.

"He hated people messing with his perfect hair. He was so mad, we didn't have sex."

Torrie claims she ended the affair in October 1996, after learning that Congressman Gary Condit was a minister's son and married. Ironically, Condit had once exploded in rage and defended all cheating husbands when Torrie informed him another married man was hitting on her at work.

"Gary went ballistic. He yelled at me, 'How can you be so selfish and judgmental? Who are you to impose your moral standards on other people?' His eyes flashed and he got all red in the face. I had never seen him so angry."

Concluding her account, Torrie remarked bluntly, "Condit was a dud in bed, not a stud — and he wasn't well-endowed. He was wham, bam, thank you ma'am, with no foreplay. He didn't care if I was pleased or not. It was so mechanical for him.

"I hear he bragged to pals about what a stud he was, how he could go all night. He was lying. He could only manage it once, then he was finished for the night. He just got on top and held my wrists down and did his thing until he was satisfied. That took about a minute and that was it."

CHASE BOTH IN HIS BODY, AND NEVER WROTE TO HER THE

CHAPTER 20

Rough sex, a serious temper, domination — all of this was part of Condit's personality, investigators were learning. But could he be violent? Could he make someone disappear? In June 2001, FBI Agent Chuck Jones met with a woman in California who provided some clues about the answers to those questions.

The woman is a close acquaintance of another former Condit lover, who is now an aide to a top California politician and wants to remain anonymous. The two friends shared many conversations about Condit. More important, the woman whom Agent Jones was meeting had a pile of X-rated letters her pal had written about Condit.

At first the letters disclosed many of the same details that had become the Condit trademark — wearing disguises including dark sunglasses and a hat, having rushed and rough sex, and showing up unexpectedly at his lover's home and getting right down to business.

"I love Mr. C. like a brother, but he doesn't have a passionate bone in his body," the lover wrote to her friend. "He rushes things. He likes to take care of business then get on to other things. How boring!

"He did spend most of the day with me, though. We went around town and he bought me lunch. But we have to go incognito everywhere we go. He has to wear dark sunglasses and a hat. He told me today that everywhere we went he knew at least half the people there — and the media would just love to get something on him.

"Maybe he treats women differently if he's in love — but this hiding-out thing is for teenagers, not me."

Agent Jones realized that Condit did not have to work hard to get this particular woman into bed. She had been aroused by his power and knew he was attracted to her, so she propositioned him in a letter mailed to his Washington condo. But the affair, which lasted for several months in 1993, never rose to the passionate heights the woman expected.

"Instead of having a nice, romantic liaison, as I had hoped, he comes to the house here one night and just screws me real quick on the couch," the woman wrote.

"It was very awkward and uncomfortable. I really thought that a man of his age would have learned how to make love to a woman, but he was like a young boy. From that point on, everything changed because he would always try to be alone in a room with me and kiss me and stuff. I hated it. Now I'm kinda scared of him. Besides, he's married.

"I'm extremely mad right now because Gary just showed up at the house knocking on the door because he knows I'm home alone. Gary always calls to find out if I'm home alone, then he'll come over. Congress is recessed . . . and now he's around all the time.

"He called a little while ago and I didn't pick up the

phone because I knew that he was checking to see if I was alone. So what does he do? He comes over anyway! Is he desperate or what?

"Normally if I don't answer the door he'll go call me from his car phone, but he didn't this time so he must know I don't want to be bothered. He's tried to be romantic by bringing me flowers and such, but I'm not interested. The whole sex thing just turned me off. You can tell how sincere a man is by the way he makes love to you — he couldn't cut the mustard."

Then the letters turned darker.

In one, the woman described Condit as being so overpowering that he threw out her back and she had to go to a chiropractor. Then the woman told her friend that she believed Condit began to stalk her and that she was terrified. Once again, exactly as had been done so effectively before, forces friendly to Condit attempted to bury the evidence.

On August 9th, the source received a letter from a lawyer.

"We have been advised that you have in your possession several confidential letters from _____ to you relating to Congressman Gary Condit," read the legal letter to the woman Agent Jones had interviewed. "As you are well aware, these letters contain specific language reflecting their personal, private, and confidential nature. In addition _____ conveyed to you verbally on several occasions the confidentiality of all her written and oral communications with you regarding Mr. Condit."

The attorney ended the letter with a threat of a lawsuit.

It dawned on the woman who met with Jones that details of her FBI interview had leaked out. She freely explained that the legal letter didn't scare her. She was cooperating because "two parents are missing their child. I wasn't going to sit back and let the Levys go through this tragedy without my help."

But something else did frighten her.

A cop in Condit's hometown of Ceres, where the congressman's brother Burl is a sergeant, chased down one of the woman's relatives who lived in the area, and relayed an explicit warning: "Tell her to stop talking to the FBI."

The woman, told of the incident by family members, explained, "I was terrified."

The thinly veiled threat brought back another memory that the woman told to Agent Jones, and given Condit's interest in motorcycling and reports that he associated with the notorious Hells Angels, the agent paid special attention.

This woman claimed that Condit had an aide who used to brag that Condit knew "powerful biker friends" who could "make people disappear with a phone call."

✳✳✳✳✳✳✳✳✳✳✳✳

Susie Borges had a three-year fling with the congressman that began in 1988. Condit was a state assemblyman, and Susie was a community worker in Modesto. Susie would eventually add yet another bizarre twist to the developing scandal.

Susie knew that Condit was married, but whenever she brought up the subject of his wife, Gary's mood darkened.

"He said she was mentally ill and that's why he couldn't bring her to public events, for fear she'd embarrass him," said Susie. "Staff [in the California capital, Sacramento] knew he was cheating on his wife."

In his early days as an assemblyman, Condit did not seem to worry about being seen with another woman. He and Susie took frequent trips to San Francisco, Los

Angeles, San Jose, and Sacramento, where Condit was rather open about their relationship.

Whenever she questioned him about the dangers of being recognized or approached by one of his constituents, Condit would respond, "I'll act like it's not me, like they're mistaken. No one will believe them. I'm like a god where I come from."

Susie said she joined Condit many nights at Paragary's, the Sacramento restaurant that is a popular hangout for politicians, their staffs, and their mistresses.

"Gary said this joint specifically catered to politicians and their mistresses," Susie recalled. "He didn't hesitate to introduce me to colleagues who were also there with their lovers. I remember how I would dirty dance with him at the restaurant. And sometimes when he was sitting down, I would throw my leg over his shoulder so he could look up my dress and he'd love it."

She recalled that Condit enjoyed taking risks by having sex with her in his Modesto office on his boardroom table, his secretary within earshot on the other side of the door.

"He loved bending me over the boardroom table, knowing he could be caught any minute," she explained. "He also liked oral sex in cars."

Susie got to see Condit's "couples kit," which he bought at a sex shop. It contained a blindfold and a pair of handcuffs. She gave them a try but admitted, "I didn't really like the submissive thing."

Condit seemed to enjoy the fact no one knew his kinky side.

"He felt completely untouchable. He'd say, 'No one would believe it anyway. My dad is a preacher and my brother is a policeman. I'm the perfect guy. I'm going to run for President one day and no one is going to ruin that.'"

Condit made sure that not even his sudden death in a questionable situation would ruin his reputation. In an elaborate plan hatched to prevent a postmortem scandal, Condit gave Susie a private number to call if he happened to die in the midst of a lovemaking session. The call would set in motion the removal of his body from a tawdry location to a final resting place more suitable for a respectable and esteemed politician.

"Gary told me this woman I was supposed to call, who was a member of his staff at the time, would know exactly which documents in his office to destroy and how to get rid of his body," explained Susie.

"Don't phone anyone from the hotel room," Condit demanded. "Take some money out of my wallet, leave me where I lay, call a cab and go to a pay phone far away. Then call the woman at that private phone number. She will know how to handle the press and what to do with my body before the police or press find out about me. Just call this woman!"

CHAPTER 21

Chantel Masengale must have stopped in her tracks when she first heard news reports about Chandra Levy. The pretty college student from Condit's home district had a romance with the congressman in the late 1990s, when she worked as an intern in his office. She never thought much more about it.

"She got dumped by Condit," said Vince Flammini, his former driver and bodyguard, "after she told him how much she loved him."

Condit, as he did with many of his lovers, gave Chantel a code name during their affair — she was to be known as "Chanandra."

****

Then there was Jennifer Baker, Chandra's friend and the third person in the now famous Blue Dog photo taken in Condit's office. She'd landed a job as an intern at his office because of that visit. Now she heard rumors circulating among the press corps that she was also involved with him.

Sickened by the gossip, she realized that by this point it was easier for most observers to assume that any intern in Condit's office had to be sleeping with the congressman.

When Chandra disappeared, Jennifer was about to start a new job back home in California with Assemblywoman Jenny Oropeza of Long Beach. Instead, she put her career on hold and joined in the hunt for her missing friend, spending long hours as a volunteer with the Sund-Carrington Foundation, the missing persons organization helping to publicize the Levy family's plight.

Jennifer admitted that her friend's disappearance haunted her.

"I can't put it out of my mind," she revealed.

To avoid the constant press hounding, Jennifer hired the lawyer Don Heller to run interference. But according to James Robinson, the attorney for Anne Marie Smith, Jennifer had another, more urgent reason for hiring an attorney.

"Jennifer Baker started to get scary phone calls, threats to keep quiet, hang-up calls," said Robinson. "Anne Marie was getting the same types of calls."

Jennifer never commented on Robinson's claims, but her mother didn't deny that her daughter had gotten threats when a reporter asked if this were true. Her voice filled with concern, she said, "She'll have to tell you about that."

****

At the end of the long list of women associated with Condit was Scarlette Parker, a retired Air Force tech sergeant. Rumor had it she was another lover, but when a *National Enquirer* reporter tracked Scarlette down in North

Carolina, he did not find another brokenhearted Condit conquest. The white-haired forty-something divorcee laughed at the suggestion that she and Condit had been involved.

She met the congressman in 1993 while stationed at Castle Air Force Base in Atwater, California, a city in Condit's congressional district. The base was closing, and Scarlette performed public relations work to help ease local residents' concerns over the economic impact of the loss.

Condit helped her handle the situation, and after she retired from the Air Force on June 1, 1994, he offered her a job as a minor staff assistant in his D.C. office. Scarlette came on board in August of that year.

"I answered the phone, arranged Blue Dog meetings for him, bought coffee, donuts."

Joleen Argentini was still employed there at the time, although just days away from the final outburst in the office.

"Joleen left just after I got there," explained Scarlette, who thinks the young woman was fabricating her affair with Condit. "I believe in my heart she may have wanted it to be more than just a friendship thing."

After reiterating that she'd never had an affair with the congressman, Scarlette revealed she had lived in Condit's D.C. condo.

"I was living in Reston, Virginia, and it was a long drive to the office."

Condit staffer Mike Dayton told her she could "rent Gary's condo," and she moved in during November 1995 and stayed for close to a year.

"I never had an affair with him," she repeated.

So where was Condit during the eleven months she occupied his apartment? "I don't know," said Scarlette.

Intent on discussing more important matters, she added her belief that Chandra was somewhere hiding, unable to face her family.

"Those interns would throw themselves at this guy's feet. They came dressed in streetwalker clothes."

To Scarlette, Gary Condit was "the most honest and above-board person and would never do anything to hurt his wife or anyone else. He wouldn't hurt a flea, and I've never seen him say a cross word to anybody. The cops are barking up the wrong tree. Gary could be President of the United States."

CHAPTER 22

Have a good day," was all Gary Condit would say to reporters as he was savaged in worldwide head-lines during July and August 2001.

"Police Seek DNA" . . . "Condit Accused of Dumping Watch Box" . . . "Authorities Search Home in D.C." . . . "Frustration Grows over Lack of Candor" . . . "Levy Family Doubts That Condit Revealed All."

Besides graphically exposing the congressman's many sexual escapades, the press was learning other damaging details about Condit. His younger brother, Darrel Condit, was a drug addict with a rap sheet thirty pages long that dated back to 1968. He'd been arrested in California and other states on charges that ranged from forging checks to a violent assault on a police officer and possession of cocaine. Cops even had to shoot him once when he tried to flee from prosecution.

"The joke around here has always been that one brother makes the law, one brother enforces the law, and one broth-er breaks the law," a former Modesto cop said, referring to

Gary Condit the congressman; his older brother, Burl, a policeman; and the youngest of the clan, Darrel.

Once a muscular six-footer who had beefed up to body-builder status while in prison, Darrel was an emaciated, drug-addled mess when a *Star* reporter found him in a run-down motel in Fort Lauderdale. When confronted, Darrel insisted his name was Stanley Buchanan. It was an alias he had been using lately when arrested.

"I know nothing about that woman, or where she is," Stanley blurted out when asked about Chandra Levy.

The real Stanley Buchanan was not surprised that his ex-prison mate had stolen his identity. He'd done time with Darrel in 1991 and the ex-con had lived with him off and on in the Sacramento area.

Darrel was always stealing to feed his drug habit, Buchanan revealed.

"The last few times he stayed with me, a lot of things went missing. I know he took an expensive jacket of mine and some of my identification. Darrel was selling the stuff to get money to buy heroin. He was always desperate for cash."

Buchanan believed that if Gary Condit wanted something done and it had a payment attached, Darrel would comply — "especially if Gary asked him."

The two brothers had remained tight despite Darrel's problems. Gary called Darrel "Little Bro" and never turned his back on the black sheep of the family. He helped pay Darrel's rent and his rehab bills, bailed him out of jail on several occasions, and welcomed him when he turned up at political functions.

When Chandra disappeared, Darrel Condit was a fugitive from a drunk-driving arrest. The news stories about the case did not help his efforts to lie low. The FBI informed

Florida's Broward County Sheriff's Department to be on the lookout for Darrel, because agents wanted to question him in relation to Chandra's disappearance.

On July 20, 2001, Darrel was arrested in the parking lot of the Red Carpet Inn in Broward County.

"We're not ruling anything out," said Washington, D.C., police Sgt. Tony O'Leary when asked if his agency would also question Darrel Condit about the Levy case. Although the DCPD kept reiterating publicly that the congressman was not officially a suspect, it was clear from the arrest of Darrel that any and all Condit links to Chandra's disappearance were now being pursued.

****

Congressman Condit eventually granted a total of four interviews to police, the last one taking place on July 27, 2001, a case-damaging twelve weeks after Chandra disappeared. Even then the authorities complained it was like pulling teeth to get Condit to answer simple questions directly. Why was he being so uncooperative?

Each day as Condit waded through the press army outside his D.C. condo, he kept his mouth tightly shut and a smile on his face, only once showing anger and raising his hand to a persistent photographer. Despite the attention, he wanted to stubbornly go about his business as if Chandra Levy had never existed.

Doing Condit's talking for him was his high-powered attorney Abbe Lowell, who held a series of press conferences to announce that Condit was cooperating with police. But the attorney's tough style, marked by aggressive and biting remarks, did not win any points with the reporters he needed to befriend.

Condit brought another player in to try and help restore his tarnished image — public relations whiz Marina Ein. It didn't take long before the expert stuck her foot in her mouth by telling at least two reporters that "Chandra Levy has her own sordid sexual history," citing an upcoming magazine article that would report that the young intern had a long and ugly history of one-night stands. Ein knowing about the article before it was published made the reporters wonder if she had something to do with its content. Not surprisingly, the information never appeared in print.

On July 13, 2001, Lowell summoned reporters to another press conference. After refusing a challenge from the Levy family to take a police-administered lie detector test, the congressman had taken a private exam, Lowell said. It proved, said the lawyer, that Condit "was not deceptive in any way" and had cooperated fully with police in the search for Chandra Levy.

Lowell claimed that three key questions were posed to the congressman:

Was Condit involved in or had he caused Chandra Levy's disappearance?

Did he harm her or cause anyone to harm her in any way?

Does he know where she can be found?

All three questions were answered with a polygraph affirming "No!"

Case closed, Lowell hinted. The press should leave Condit alone, he said, lecturing the members of the media in a condescending tone.

"The more time that is spent on Congressman Condit, the more you're diverting attention away from the only thing that matters here — finding Chandra Levy."

The announcement backfired in a big way.

Police had not been told beforehand that Condit was taking the exam. Chief Terry Gainer, although not questioning the credentials of the polygraph examiner — former FBI agent Barry Colvert — commented that the way in which the test was given was advantageous to Condit.

"We wanted to ask the questions," explained Gainer. "I've never been involved in a polygraph exam . . . where the polygrapher didn't want to know the facts [from the police]. So this is a bit self-serving."

Attorney Billy Martin also indicated that Bob and Susan Levy were not satisfied with Condit's polygraph test. In calling again for Condit to take an exam administered by the police or the FBI, Martin said, "Since he made these private arrangements while we and the authorities were trying to reach an agreement on the questions to be asked, the Levy family feels that Congressman Condit's actions were not in the spirit of cooperating with the Levy family."

As criticism mounted, Condit decided to finally open his mouth to a national audience, agreeing to sit down for an interview with ABC's Connie Chung on August 23, 2001. A home audience of 24 million people tuned in to get their first close look at a politician who just four months earlier was hardly known beyond his home district. When the thirty-minute interview concluded, it was clear Condit had made a huge mistake.

Coming across as a pompous politician, Condit steadfastly refused to admit he had an affair with Chandra. It looked all the worse, considering that by this time Anne Marie Smith had gone public, Linda Zamsky had spoken to the *Washington Post*, and Condit's admissions during the third police interview had been leaked. Furthermore, Condit never apologized to Chandra's parents for his indiscretions with their daughter.

In reference to the intimate details that Linda Zamsky revealed about Chandra's affair with Condit, the congressman, dancing around the real issue, said, "Chandra is not here to defend herself. So I don't know why the aunt would say that."

Regarding his roundabout answers to Susan Levy on the phone when she called him at the time Chandra disappeared, Condit said, "My job was to console and do what I could to be helpful. But I never lied to Mrs. Levy at all. I'm sorry if she misunderstood the conversations."

Condit went on to call Anne Marie Smith a liar for saying he asked her to sign an affidavit denying their affair. The affidavit was "a statement," as he called it, "that a lawyer sent to another lawyer. I did not have anything to do with that."

Of Anne Marie herself, he said he was "puzzled by, uh, people who take advantage of tragedy, a missing person that they don't even know."

As for the infamous watch box incident, he said, "Uh, the watch box had nothing to do with Chandra Levy. I did not take anything out of the apartment before or after the search. The watch box . . . was trash that I threw away." Condit was again bobbing and weaving. "There was nothing to it."

He admitted that the watch was a gift from a staffer but did not identify Joleen Argentini by name.

Did he have a relationship with her? Connie Chung wanted to know.

"I did not," replied Condit.

As a crew filmed the Condit family walking pleasantly through a grove of trees, according to an observer, "Gary's wife Carolyn briefly put her arm around her husband's waist but almost as quickly as she touched him, she jerked her arm back. It's as if she really didn't want to have any physical contact with her husband. She smiled for an instant for the camera, but it seemed clear she was smiling to cover up the deep hurt she felt."

Carolyn then watched Gary's performance on a monitor. Several times during the interview, when Condit was pressed by Chung to admit his affair with Chandra, Carolyn could be seen muttering to the screen, according to the observer.

"The hardest moment for the lady came when Gary referred to her as 'that woman' as he told Connie Chung about the state of their marriage. He told Chung, 'I'll stay married to that woman as long as she'll have me.' You could tell the words cut Carolyn like a knife."

Commentators crucified Condit in print and on the airwaves in the days following the interview.

"I was yelling 'liar' at the television," said Joanne Tittle, a close friend of the Levys, echoing sentiments expressed across the country.

Political colleagues distanced themselves quickly.

"I think [the interview] fell way short. It all adds to the general perception that politics are no good and politicians are a bunch of bums," said powerful House Minority Leader Richard Gephardt of Missouri. He called his Democratic colleague's lack of candor "disturbing and wrong."

As September 2001 began, things grew even worse for Gary Condit. In possibly the ultimate insult, his public relations guru quit on him. Marina Ein must have felt his image was beyond repair.

CHAPTER 23

The names Chandra Levy and Gary Condit vanished from the news with the tragic events of September 11, 2001. The satellite television trucks headed out of Modesto, and reporters stopped following the congressman. Chandra Levy "REWARD" flyers came down, replaced by "WANTED" posters for Al Qaeda leaders.

The week before the terrorist attacks, local officials from Chandra's hometown had flown to Washington, D.C., to get updates on the case from D.C. police.

Those meetings were scrapped.

"September 11th virtually pushed the Levy case off the map for most people," said Kelly Huston, a spokesperson for the Stanislaus County Sheriff's Department.

On that horrible day, Susan Levy, whose own world had crumbled months before the Twin Towers, prepared for a flight to Chicago to appear on Oprah, after which she would travel to New York for an appearance on the *Today* show. She needed to keep the interest in her daughter alive.

A phone call from a friend saved Susan the trip — the

World Trade Center and the Pentagon were in flames.

"The whole world changed," said Susan. "First for us, when all of a sudden — poof — Chandra disappeared. It was like some kind of terrorist invaded our family and we've been at war. Then it happened to the world, when terrorists invaded and thousands of people disappeared. I felt helpless. When this happened, it doubled my grief."

Susan considered running a newspaper ad to say that her family felt for all the victims of September 11th, but ultimately rejected the idea, and instead privately prayed for the thousands of lost souls.

As letters laced with deadly anthrax poison spread more fear across the nation, Susan began wearing thick rubber gloves to open her mail. In an ironic twist, the Levys were receiving messages of sympathy addressed simply to "Robert and Susan Levy, General Delivery, Modesto, California," at a time when postal authorities were warning people to avoid exactly that kind of delivery.

"The whole country is shocked and hurt over the terrorist attack, and we feel awful for all those people, too," said Chandra's brother, Adam. "But we've been shocked and sad over Chandra for what feels like forever.

"But how do we deal with a national issue like that, when we have such horrible international issues to deal with? It's all crazy."

September 12th was a benchmark day for Gary Condit. On that date twelve years earlier, he was elected to Congress in a special election to fill a vacant seat. He had been unbeatable ever since.

Now the pundits unanimously called it "Mission Impossible" for him to seek an eighth term in the House when he came up for reelection in November 2002. Chandra Levy's disappearance hovered over him, and he had come across badly on national TV during his interview with Connie Chung.

What's more, state lawmakers reconfigured his home district in California. Loyal and longtime supporters were no longer eligible to cast their ballots for Gary Condit. Residents living within his new district knew him only as "that married politician whose girlfriend had mysteriously vanished."

"Maybe if Condit was running against Mullah Omar, he'd at least have a shot at it," joked California political analyst Tony Quinn.

Before September 11th, Chad and Cadee Condit went on record saying that they preferred that their father not seek reelection and that their mom "probably" felt the same way.

Gary Condit did not.

With the nation's attention now on Afghanistan, Condit scraped together only 2,543 voter signatures, a few hundred signatures shy of the minimum 3,000 required to put his name on the ballot. It was an embarrassment, but a check written to the government for $221 dollars covered the difference. On December 7, 2001, forty-five minutes before the deadline for federal candidates in California, he strode into the Stanislaus County Courthouse and filed the necessary paperwork for the 2002 election.

"I'm running," he eagerly told reporters.

What lay ahead was a campaign to win a March 5th Democratic primary against five opponents who had lined up to challenge the beleaguered politician. Condit hoped voters would look at his record and not his troubles.

"I've been married thirty-four years," he mentioned in an interview outlining his qualities. "I don't drink, don't smoke, don't party. I have received thousands of letters from people who understand that the media has trampled on my civil liberties and privacy and has tried to lynch me in the press. It's just nonsense."

His campaign was a disaster. *The New York Times Sunday Magazine* writer Frank Bruni followed Condit as he wandered through his district, desperately trying to keep the campaign on a higher ground. He still wanted to avoid any mention of "that missing intern."

Bruni described a stop at a local Starbucks to meet with voters that turned into a typical fiasco.

"One of the issues that's definitely important to voters is your credibility," a reporter insisted. Condit went silent and turned away. His head bobbed left and right, looking for someone to save him. Still the reporter persisted, "A lot of people think you lied to the Washington police."

Condit desperately tried to find someone without a notepad or camera. Thankfully, a heavy-set, bearded man with a smile on his face approached. Condit was relieved when the apparent supporter asked about district matters.

"I have only one other question," the man then said. "Where did you bury the body?"

Condit blurted out, "You're a joke."

"No," the man replied, "you're a joke."

It was a scene repeated over and over again as signs reading "Fire the Liar" and "Gary's Scary" greeted him during the campaign.

All the while, Condit continued to blame others for his personal problems. As Bruni wrote, the congressman believed that the Washington, D.C., police accused him of obstruction because they had a horrible record for finding missing people. Connie Chung focused too much on Chandra, refusing to let him talk about the inaccuracies of the malicious press corps. Other politicians were too weak to stand by him. Condit simply believed that he was fighting a righteous battle, and ultimately fellow members of Congress would respect a man who survived adversity.

Bruni recounted that Condit went to see the movie *Ali*, starring Will Smith, and was enlightened by the story of the boxing champion who had stood by his religious convictions and refused to fight in the Vietnam War.

"There are some messages in that," Bruni quotes Condit as saying. "Here's a guy — everything had turned on him. He stood up for principle, and the country was going the other way. They caught up with him, eventually. In the short term, it looked like he was doomed. But in the long term, he kept his faith and he kept his principled position, and now look at what we think of Ali."

"You know, we went through quite an ordeal, a storm." Condit's father said, reaching into his bag of sermons to deliver some words on his son's behalf. Only fifty guests had showed up for the fund-raising buffet. "Well, it wasn't a storm — it was an Oklahoma tornado."

"Lord, when that day comes," Adrian Condit bellowed, looking up towards the heavens. "When we go to the polls and cast votes, I'm going to expect Gary to come out on top. I'm going to believe that, because we know that you're always for those who lift up the holy banner of right and good and love and peace."

Condit's son Chad was simultaneously comparing his family's fight to a Mafia battle, saying, "We've gone to the mattresses."

Bruni added later that Condit was "a guy who's become so convinced of his own victimization that he seems to have lost sight of his hand in it. He believes that . . . the affair with Chandra Levy is his own business, not something that has any implications on his public service."

Congressional colleagues and longtime supporters did not agree. Paul Warda, who had lent his walnut ranch to Condit for the Connie Chung interview, no longer spoke out on behalf of his friend. California Representative Nancy Pelosi, the second-highest-ranking Democrat in the House, went mum on Condit's reelection bid, as did former Ohio Congressman John Kasich, the same man who had jumped into the mosh pit alongside Condit at a Pearl Jam concert.

Desperate, Condit finally brought up Chandra's name in the hopes he could salvage his career. He claimed his reelection was in fact "the best thing for the Levy family." In Washington, he would use his power to keep the authorities searching for the missing intern.

On March 5, 2002, former friend and staff member State Assemblyman Dennis Cardoza soundly defeated Condit in the primary. Condit would stay in office until December 31st, but his thirty-year political career was over. He would be replaced by the winner of the November runoff between Cardoza and Republican State Senator Dick Monteith.

Outside his home in Ceres, Condit met reporters and thanked voters who supported him. About fifteen minutes after his brief statement, the sprinklers went on, dousing television crews and photographers.

The Levys' private investigator, Joe McCann, later recalled the promise the congressman had made before the March 5th primary — that if he won the election it would be the best thing for the Levy family, because he would be in a position to keep the pressure on authorities to find Chandra.

"Well, you can tell Gary I will always be investigating her disappearance," McCann assured. "And he can either feel comfortable or uncomfortable with that."

CHAPTER 24

On March 6, 2002, Gary Condit crept back to Washington a beaten man. His campaign for the Democratic nomination and a shot at an eighth term in Congress had failed. The affair with Chandra Levy proved to be one affair too many.

As a congressman, Condit had done many good things for the Central Valley. His efforts to preserve prime agricultural land aided the farmers and grape growers in the region. He worked hard at eliminating unfunded mandates imposed on local agencies by the federal government. He won extra law enforcement resources for his district in the war on drugs and sponsored a bill to protect consumers from deceptive mailings and sweepstakes. Condit's Blue Dog Democrats bucked their party leadership if they believed a Republican cause worthy, and President Bush openly courted the group during his election campaign.

The few close friends that Condit had left, instead of planning the next "Condit Country" event, wondered what he would be able to do next.

"I've heard him say that he's not afraid of work, but I wondered what work," said Ronald Ashlock, a well-known labor leader and supporter in Condit's home district in California. "The only work he's ever done is to serve the public. He doesn't have a big bank account. He doesn't own a lot."

Condit himself had joked that if he lost the primary, he could work as a welder, a job he once held before politics beckoned, but his situation was dire. He had dipped into his campaign funds to pay the attorney Abbe Lowell just over $100,000, and the public relations specialist Marina Ein put him out another $17,000. He eventually sold his D.C. condo in the Adams Morgan neighborhood with little trouble for $166,000, dumping the $50,000 profit from the sale into his campaign coffers. According to the 2001 year-end report he filed with the Federal Election Commission, he had $73,000 in cash on hand.

Based on his congressional salary of $145,100 a year, Condit would get a federal pension of no more than $31,500 a year. There was a state pension he had earned as a California assemblyman that would contribute $12,000 more. That added up to a sad legacy for a man who years earlier boasted to Susie Borges that he'd be President one day. Condit had become accustomed to a certain lifestyle that $43,500 a year would not support.

Now his name had become totally synonymous with "unfaithful."

"Ceres is as old-fashioned and traditional as any place," said a friend of the Condits. "So having an affair with a girl who's the same age as your daughter is a big sin.

"Gary lost the election and now he's about to be unemployed. People here loved Gary before Chandra disappeared. He had a job in Congress for life.

"His family lived in a modest home, but it was more than comfortable enough for them. They had every reason to believe that they would stay in that house for years to come.

"All that is gone," the friend went on, outlining how the future held only uncertainty. "They have money problems from the campaign and legal bills. Gary's job prospects are far dimmer than Carolyn expected, and he is the punchline of late-night TV jokes. That's just got to hurt."

Condit's official congressional Web site, rarely updated since Chandra's disappearance, was also looking more like a joke for late-night TV.

"Read what these newspapers are saying about Gary Condit," one page stated. If you clicked on the link, what you got was a seven-year-old article from the *Washington Post* headlined "A Power Broker Comes of Age."

"Condit pads around his Washington office in slippers and a sweater like a Central Valley incarnation of Jimmy Carter," the article read, "but he rides a Harley when he goes back home every weekend to see his family."

And in an eerie observation, the reporter went on, "He keeps a bicycle stashed in his office to take off through Rock Creek Park during legislative lulls."

Keeping with tradition, the Web site notably still invited young people to seek internship opportunities in the congressman's office.

The most recent addition to Condit's Web site was a group photograph with the caption "Members of the Subcommittee on Terrorism and Homeland Security Tour Ground Zero."

Condit had been named to the subcommittee created in the days after September 11th to improve the nation's vigilance in the war on terrorism. In light of Condit's situation, the appointment drew criticism from a host of political commentators.

The photo showed Representatives David Obey, Jane Harman, Sanford Bishop, and, in sunglasses, Condit. The expression on Bishop's face seemed to say, "How did I wind up next to Condit?"

Standing behind the four, in a hard hat, was former President Clinton, who also looked like he didn't want to get anywhere near Condit.

Clinton had been dubbed the "Comeback Kid" for his ability to rebound from his indiscretions and scandalous liaison with intern Monica Lewinsky. Gary Condit, however, was no comeback kid. The problems that arose from his affair with intern Chandra Levy were still on the front burner and getting worse.

The very day Condit returned to the capital to start packing up his office, Bob and Susan Levy once again stepped up the pressure in the hopes of learning Chandra's true fate. Using Condit's loss in the primaries as an opportunity to speak to the press, Bob stood outside his Modesto home and said, "Congressman Condit has pledged to do everything he could to help us find our daughter. We ask him to keep those promises and talk to our investigators and help us find our daughter."

"The most important thing Condit can do today to keep this investigation moving," their attorney, Billy Martin, echoed, "is to tell us all he knows or suspects and to do so now."

Condit was still ducking the requests from the Levys, but he couldn't ignore a federal grand jury now looking into Chandra's disappearance. Authorities, angered at his elusive behavior, wanted answers. They had subpoenaed datebooks, calendar entries, memos and other documents from the congressman four months earlier. Then Condit himself was slapped with a subpoena, requiring him to appear before the grand jury. The word was that members of his staff, along with Chandra's friends and acquaintances, would also be called as witnesses.

The federal prosecutors had a lot of questions on their minds. Did Condit hinder the investigation by lying to police or other authorities? Did he actually urge Anne Marie Smith to commit perjury by signing an affidavit denying their affair? Did members of his staff do the same? All of that could amount to serious obstruction of justice and subornation of perjury charges.

Condit had a new hired gun, top Los Angeles celebrity attorney Mark Geragos, who divided his time between representing the congressman and actress Winona Ryder, who was facing shoplifting charges. Geragos served as a lone supporter of Condit during many talk show appearances in the weeks after Chandra disappeared, even going one-on-one defending Condit to Chandra's Aunt Linda when she called in to the Larry King Show.

At one point during the investigation, Geragos had asserted that speculation that the congressman may have been involved with Chandra Levy's disappearance was merely "wild theories and speculation."

Geragos was an experienced "talking head" who freely welcomed any opportunity to grab quality air-time. On the night of April 18th, as actor Robert Blake was arrested for murdering his wife, Bonny Lee Bakley, Geragos somehow escaped an L.A. highway nightmare to rush to the CNN studios. There, he quickly joined in an interview with Blake's attorney, Harland Braun.

Geragos surely knew millions were tuning in by the second to watch Blake get hauled away in cuffs, and it was a perfect situation for the lawyer to gain more recognition. The camera constantly cut to Geragos as he eloquently explained his colleague's options regarding Blake.

Now Geragos tried to work his patented magic on the federal grand jury, before which Condit appeared on Friday, April 12th. Condit should have been grilled all day according to many experts, but his appearance lasted less than an hour. Geragos had once again done his client well.

Condit received assurances from prosecutors that he would not be asked questions about his sex life with Chandra. The twenty-three-member grand jury was told to focus only on obstruction of justice charges and whether Condit urged other people to perjure themselves on his behalf. It was unusual, but not unheard of.

Private investigator Jeff Green, a former D.C. homicide detective, explained that questioning was probably limited during Condit's appearance because "he was a sitting member of Congress. It wouldn't be unusual for his lawyer to sit down with prosecutors and say the focus has to be this, and for prosecutors to agree."

After all, Chandra was still just a missing person — there was still no solid evidence she was the victim of a crime.

Despite their instructions, the grand jurors tried to play hardball with Condit.

"They wanted to know about Condit's relationship with Chandra and asked a lot of questions about their sex life," said an investigative source. "But Condit wouldn't answer. He had to keep repeating that he couldn't answer some of their questions.

"He was definitely rehearsed. It looked like his attorney went through everything with him. His answers were cautious and slow. He paused after every question. The U.S. Attorney questioned Condit first, and then the individual jurors began to ask questions. One after the other, they asked about Condit and his relationship with Chandra. The prosecutor had to tell them they could only ask questions pertaining to obstruction of justice or subornation of perjury."

One focus of the grand jury session was Condit's alibi for his whereabouts on the day Chandra disappeared, particularly his statement to police that he went to a chiropractor at 5 p.m., but couldn't remember the doctor's name or address.

Asked about Condit's memory loss, his attorney Geragos, always quick to divert attention elsewhere, joked to a reporter that all must be well with the country's war on terrorism if Condit was back in the news.

Then Geragos added, "I can almost categorically deny" that Condit couldn't provide the name of the doctor or his address.

Told that an "almost" categorical denial amounted to no denial at all, Geragos promised to get the name of the doctor and the address from Condit.

Further calls from the reporter to Geragos went unreturned.

✳✳✳✳✳✳✳✳✳✳✳✳

On May 1, 2002, the anniversary of Chandra's disappearance, fifty people holding candles gathered in front of the Newport, the Washington building where the intern had rented a studio apartment.

Many of them wore buttons printed with the question, "Where is Chandra?"

The Levys were there, with Susan reading a passage from the Old Testament about redemption. When she had finished, she said simply, "I would like to tell you that this has been so hard, so hard."

The emotional toll manifested itself physically. In her grief, Susan Levy was finding it difficult to control the auditory dyslexia that had always plagued her, and as a result words and conversations sometimes became mixed up in her mind.

"She'd be at the dining room table, talking a mile a minute in disjointed phrases," said Don Vance, a family friend. "Oh, isn't this food wonderful? . . . Pass me that, please . . . Did you see the TV showed that horrible picture of Chandra again, the one that makes her look like a slut? . . . Aren't these vegetables delicious?. . .Why can't they find her? . . . Pass me that, please."

Watching Susan go on and on like that and Bob crying was heart-wrenching, said Vance. He couldn't bear to see them suffering so.

Grief wasn't the only emotion tormenting Susan. She had come to feel hatred for Gary Condit, a feeling that went against her very being. "Susan is a very spiritual, mystical woman, and hating someone goes against all of that," said a friend.

"She's attended mystical healing sessions and often practices yoga as a means to relieve the tension and pain. But she says all of the praying and meditating is ruined by thoughts of Condit that keep creeping into her mind. She absolutely loathes him."

The day before the memorial service outside Chandra's building, Bob Levy decided to be more frank about his belief that Condit had something to do with his daughter's disappearance. In an appearance on the *Today* show, he bluntly told Matt Lauer, "We believe that she went to meet him [on the day she disappeared]."

"Total suffering," is how the son of Don Vance described Bob's state of mind.

"I was with him at dinner and he'd break down in the middle," said Eric Vance. "He is lost in his obsession to find Chandra."

CHAPTER 25

On the morning of May 22, 2002, Executive Assistant Police Chief Gainer was enjoying scrambled eggs and orange juice in a diner in the Washington, D.C. area. With him was a *Washington Post* reporter, and the Chandra Levy case inevitably came up.

Between bites, Gainer explained that the investigators needed a break: Either someone had to provide a tip, "or we find the body."

Across town, a man and his dog methodically worked their way through the tangled vegetation along Broad Branch Creek in Rock Creek Park.

Hidden by tall trees and dense undergrowth from the windows of the mansions bordering the creek, the man let the animal run loose, sniffing and scratching at piles of dead leaves.

Their quarry on this sunny May morning were the box turtles that inhabit the park. The man would later tell police that he was "just looking" for turtles. It is illegal to take the creatures out of the park, but they make attractive pets with their drab brown shells contrasting with the vivid red, orange and yellow streaks on their heads.

At the foot of a steep incline, the dog began pawing at the ground. As the man approached, he saw what appeared to be the top of a turtle shell protruding above leaves and twigs. He knelt and began brushing aside earth and debris. A moment later he recoiled in horror as he recognized a human skull.

The man quickly ran up the hill in a panic, emerging from the forest just above Broad Branch Creek. He leaped from boulder to boulder to cross a small stream and spotted a house under construction. "I have to call the police," he gasped to the first worker he saw.

The man was handed a cell phone, and shaking uncontrollably, he struggled to dial a number. Another worker finally dialed 911 for him. The man blurted out the story of his grisly find to the emergency dispatch operator.

It was just after 9:30 when Gainer's pager went off. Still enjoying his breakfast with the *Post* reporter, he elected to ignore it. A moment later it went off again and he checked into the station.

After 386 days, Chandra Levy was no longer a missing person.

✳✳✳✳✳✳✳✳✳✳✳✳✳

A U.S. Parks police officer was at the area within twenty minutes, and was led to the site by the turtle hunter. They were soon joined by dozens of D.C. cops, who fanned out through the area, some climbing the dense undergrowth and up the 35-degree wooded hill. For most, it was familiar territory. Rock Creek Park, after all, had been searched not long ago.

About 100 feet above where the skull was discovered, investigators stopped abruptly. There, clearly visible near a tree, lay an intact spine. Soon other bones, some gnawed and moved by foxes or raccoons, were discovered lying in the same general area. Close by was a Walkman radio and faded clothes including Reebok tennis shoes, a red sports bra, panties, and a University of Southern California T-shirt.

At the foot of a tree was the first evidence that this was no accident — a pair of stretch leggings, each leg knotted at the ankles as if they had been used to bind the victim's wrists and feet.

The location of the spine indicated the victim's final resting place. The skull, detectives theorized, had detached after months of exposure to the elements and simply rolled down the hill. Looking up from the area where the spine and clothes lay, they saw that the steep incline went up another 25 to 30 yards, and then leveled off. Beyond that was quiet Ridge Road with its picnic areas and small parking lots.

Dr. Jonathan Arden, the D.C. medical examiner, arrived to survey the scene. As he turned over the skull, he saw that the teeth were intact, lending hope for a fast identification. Unlike other body parts, teeth are extremely resistant to decomposition and, when compared with a person's dental chart, can provide as positive an ID as a fingerprint or DNA.

Dr. Arden drove back to his office at D.C. General Hospital in southeast Washington with the evidence in a container on the backseat of his car. In his lab, he X-rayed the skull and clipped the film to a light screen. Next to that X-ray he placed another — the last one taken by Chandra Levy's dentist before she vanished.

By now the small room was full of police officers and FBI agents, as well as other federal investigators. Senior detectives Ralph Durant and Lawrence Kennedy, who had led the long search for Chandra, knew whose remains they had discovered as soon as they saw the USC T-shirt. They remembered that Chandra had studied for her master's degree at the University of Southern California. With everyone else, they waited for their fear to be officially confirmed.

With his back to the room, Dr. Arden peered at the left X-ray, then the right. He made a second, then a third visual examination.

Finally he turned around.

"It's her," he said.

With these words, the thirteen-month-long hunt for Chandra Levy ended, and the search for her killer began.

****

At almost the very moment their daughter's remains were found, Bob and Susan Levy were preparing to speak to Oprah Winfrey via satellite. They were at home in Modesto, and the talk show host was in her studio in Chicago.

For Bob and Susan, it was one more chance to try to keep alive the public's interest in their daughter.

"We really hope that she is alive," Bob told Oprah as they began taping. "It doesn't seem likely. But as parents, we have to maintain that hope."

"Do you think that Gary Condit knows what happened?" Oprah asked Susan.

"Oh yes," the mother replied. "I think he does."

A half-hour later at 8:30 a.m. Pacific time, after the TV

technicians had left the Levy house, the phone rang. It was D.C. Police Chief Charles Ramsey, and his voice was cracking with emotion so badly that Susan put him on the speaker phone and called for Bob to join her. They held hands as he told them that the remains of a woman had been found in Rock Creek Park.

Chief Ramsey called again at 11 a.m. to say they were still uncertain about an official identification, but tests were being conducted. Finally, just before 3 p.m., attorney Billy Martin was given the heart-wrenching task of passing the awful news on to Bob and Susan.

CHAPTER 26

On May 28, 2002, Dr. Jonathan Arden held a news conference on the grass outside his office. He stepped to a podium jammed with microphones.

"The remains recovered last week in Rock Creek Park were positively identified by the Office of the Chief Medical Examiner as Chandra Ann Levy, by comparison of dental X-rays. Her death has been certified today by this office. The cause of death has been certified as 'undetermined,' and the manner of death as 'homicide.'

"Prior to this press conference, I spoke with Mr. Billy Martin, the attorney for the Levy family, and have disclosed these results, and offered condolences to the Levy family."

Taking questions from the press, Arden spoke in the blunt terms of a man who deals with death on a daily basis. "I had less to work with than I would like," he admitted, referring to the sparse skeletal remains.

The homicide ruling had been made on what he called the "prime facts" of the case: The remote location in the park where her body was found and a pair of stretch leggings that had been knotted.

Arden said the condition of Chandra's remains was "consistent with the time frame in which she disappeared."

"We are one of the best police agencies in the world and we will solve this case," Police Chief Ramsey promised.

But with a poor homicide closure rate — just forty-eight percent — his department was taking some heat. A quicker discovery of the body would have yielded more clues about the way Chandra died, the experts noted.

"We searched what was a reasonable area to find the body. I would say we searched most of Rock Creek Park," said Ramsey, trying to counter the criticism. He then admitted, "The bottom line is . . . we didn't find her."

The police spent another week examining the hillside using crime scene experts, cadaver dogs, and even anthropologists from the Smithsonian Institute. Finding nothing, they abandoned the site.

On June 6th, Joe McCann and Dwayne Stanton, the investigators hired by the Levys, visited the slope where Chandra's remains were found and using a rake, uncovered her tibia bone, the second-largest bone in the human body. It lay just 25 yards from the spot where her skull had been discovered.

Police Chief Ramsey closed off the site again, and Chandra's left femur bone was found.

★★★★★★★★★★★★

Ralph Durant and Lawrence Kennedy, the DCPD detectives assigned to the Chandra Levy case from the start, had felt instinctively that this was no random act of murder. They were convinced that she must have known her killer.

Although the steep hillside in Rock Creek Park where her remains lay for 13 months was the coldest crime scene imaginable, there were definite clues that lent credence to that theory.

For one thing, Chandra's portable Walkman, the headphones still attached to it, was sitting neatly on a rock. Her panties were dangling on the branch of a bush, as if they had been hung there to protect them from getting dirty on the ground. These items indicated the possibility that Chandra went voluntarily into the woods to engage in a sexual tryst with someone she knew, expecting to eventually reclaim her belongings and walk back out.

A pair of sunglasses was recovered, along with a tube of lipstick. Why would Chandra have brought a lipstick with her for a casual or random stroll through the park? Along with the Walkman and the panties, this item countered any argument that Chandra spent her last moments frantically trying to defend herself from an attacker. A more likely scenario was that she made a quick touchup to look her best for a special someone she went to meet that fateful day.

The Reebok tennis shoes confirmed that Chandra was not out for a run. The footwear she wore when she jogged on treadmills at her health club was back in her apartment.

Family members and her close friend, Jennifer Baker, stated emphatically that Chandra did not like to exercise in Rock Creek Park. Jennifer even told John Walsh of *America's Most Wanted* that Chandra was fearful about going into the park. Only at the urging of someone she knew would Chandra venture in, detectives were being told.

Chandra's hyoid bone, which is located on the front of the neck about an inch from the top of her chest, indicated the possibility that she had been strangled. In performing his medical examination, Dr. Arden found that the hyoid was slightly damaged, not fractured, as would be the case if Chandra's killer strangled her with his hands wrapped around her throat, his thumbs putting pressure on the fragile bone.

A damaged hyoid could, however, indicate other forms of strangulation, according to Hal Sherman, a former top New York City crime scene detective who has investigated nearly two thousand homicides.

The killer, said Sherman, might have choked Chandra to death from behind, using a stick or baton, or a forearm wrapped around her throat. "It's like the illegal choke holds that cops aren't suppose to use," added Sherman. "This would damage but not necessarily fracture the hyoid."

Sherman said that one would need more than bones to be positive, however. Hemorrhaging in the eyes, for instance, is a sign of strangling by rope, so-called "ligature strangulation" in police parlance. But decomposition was long complete when Chandra's remains were found.

Then there were the leggings, discovered near the base of a tree. They revealed that Chandra was most likely being restrained when she died. Each leg was knotted separately at the ankle as if the leggings were used to bind her wrists and feet, or maybe even to tie her to the tree, her face pressed up against the trunk. Most of her spine was still intact, and its position on the ground disclosed that Chandra was face down when her killer finished with her. Investigators wondered if this was a sexual bondage situation, the killer assaulting her from behind before taking her life.

Chandra's clothing and the other personal items found at the crime scene were sent to FBI labs for analysis. There appeared to be dried fluid on the crotch area of the leggings, which would require a close look by the forensic scientists.

Police had also fanned out in the park to collect bits of trash strewn in an area between the precise site where Chandra's body was found and the Klingle Mansion. Among the garbage collected and sent to the FBI lab was a discarded Baskin-Robbins ice cream container. On the day she disappeared, Chandra had looked up the location of the mansion and the nearest Baskin-Robbins on her laptop before heading out of her apartment.

"The cops stopped by and asked if Chandra came in," said the shop manager, Chairod Raungtriphop. "My employees didn't remember her but we're a popular place. She could have easily come in. We're near the park and lots of people take ice cream there. Yeah, it's a romantic gesture, ice cream to share with a boyfriend or girlfriend."

Suddenly those last few hours of Chandra's final day became all the more important to investigators. This was looking like a crime of passion executed by a lover. Who could that person have been? Who was Chandra seeing?

Her family and investigators state there was only one man in the intern's life they knew of — Congressman Gary Condit.

"Someone in her personal life did this," said former FBI profiler Greg McCrary, echoing the sentiments of the investigators looking into the homicide.

If Chandra did venture into the woods voluntarily, her last moments were spent in certain horror, passion having turned into punishment.

But if it was Gary Condit, what would his motive be? Once again we have to piece together Chandra's last days for a theory.

Recall that on Sunday, April 29th, right after making one

of her many calls to Condit, Chandra had called her Aunt Linda and left a message on her answering machine.

"I have some really big news," she had said excitedly.

What was the big news?

Some investigators have come to believe that Chandra might have been pregnant.

Sven Jones, Chandra's pal at the Bureau of Prisons, recalled, "Maybe a month before she disappeared we took the train home together. She told me she was having female problems. I wasn't sure whether she was talking about a pregnancy."

The question was taken seriously enough that investigators ultimately asked the congressman himself if Chandra had told him she was expecting a child.

"No," he replied coldly.

Gary Condit had lost his touch when it came to discarding inconvenient women. Did he finally realize that he had slept with one woman too many, and this time he was about to be ruined? Pregnant or not, Chandra Levy would have done anything to stay with the powerful congressman.

"His mistake was that he underestimated how tenacious Chandra was," said UCLA psychiatrist Dr. Carole Lieberman. "He'd been able to get rid of the other women more easily."

"I've been with more than a thousand other women," Condit had bragged to Vince Flammini, his driver and bodyguard. Continued Flammini, "Once they fell head over heels in love, he'd say, 'Screw you, baby. I'm outta here!'"

"Condit didn't count on Chandra's sincerity or the strength of her romantic fantasies and her determination to turn them into reality," Lieberman added. "Unlike his other lovers, Chandra didn't see there being anyone else for her."

CHAPTER 27

Sometimes the process of elimination is the best way for a detective to arrive at a conclusion. Before they were convinced that an acquaintance had murdered Chandra Levy, DCPD investigators Ralph Durant and Lawrence Kennedy had put a tremendous amount of legwork into their hunt for the missing intern.

Thanks to the help of their fellow cops, nearly all of Washington's sixteen hundred cabbies had been questioned to see if they gave a ride to Chandra the day she disappeared. It was a long shot, one of many investigators had to pursue, but worth a try. An extensive list of known sexual offenders were also tracked down and grilled, as were convicted predators arrested for assaults on young women.

"There were quite a few nutcases who hung around Chandra's neighborhood and followed women," said a law enforcement source, explaining the challenges officials faced. "One was a British man who kept pestering a woman who lived very close to Chandra's apartment. He got a long, hard look."

One convicted felon, Ingmar Guandique, came under intense scrutiny after demonstrating his true vicious personality. The twenty-year-old immigrant from El Salvador attacked two women in Rock Creek Park during the weeks following Chandra's disappearance, and the judge who sentenced him for the assaults described Guandique as a dangerous predator. His acts were all the more suspect in light of Chandra Levy's murder.

Guandique's first recorded encounter with Washington police was on May 7, 2001, six days after Chandra disappeared. At 1:15 p.m. that day, Tomasa Orellana and her nine-year-old daughter, Hazel, returned to their D.C. apartment on Somerset Place NW, near the eastern edge of Rock Creek Park.

Tomasa told police later that she "heard a noise" coming from her bedroom and found a man "hiding in the corner." She said, "I screamed as he walked toward me, his hands stretched out. My heart was pounding like a drum and my whole body was shaking."

Hazel was frozen in fear.

"I saw his hand in front of him and I thought he had a gun. That's how it happens in the movies. The man jumps out with a gun or a knife. I was scared and didn't know what was going to happen."

Fortunately, Tomasa's screams sent the intruder running from the apartment.

Police called to the scene found that the deadbolt on the front door of the apartment had been broken to gain entry. Tomasa told them a gold ring was missing from her home and described the man as "a Hispanic male wearing a striped yellow shirt, and black pants."

Minutes later they found Guandique nearby, who not only fit the specific description but also had an incriminating gold ring in his pocket. Tomasa positively identified Guandique as the man she saw in her apartment.

Guandique, who does not speak English, was interviewed by a Spanish-speaking officer. He revealed he had lived in the Washington area for a year and a half and had been employed for only three months as a carpenter. The next day, Guandique checked off a box on a release form that represented a promise to "refrain from committing any criminal offense." A judge cut him loose.

Six days later, Guandique was stalking Rock Creek Park, and his victim on May 14th became thirty-year-old university professor Halle Shilling.

"I went to Rock Creek Park for a run at about 6:30 in the evening," Shilling later wrote to the sentencing judge in the case, attempting to make sure Guandique received an appropriate and harsh sentence. "I was wearing a bright yellow Walkman radio with earphones and started jogging from the parking lot at Pierce Mill. About 200 yards into my run, at the next parking lot, I noticed a young Hispanic guy sitting on the curb watching as I ran by. I made a mental note, but kept running."

Guandique ran after her, keeping pace for five or six minutes.

"As I slowed, this runner jumped me from behind," Shilling explained in horrifying detail. "We wrestled and it became clear he was physically attacking me. I twisted around, in the ensuing moment, and realized my attacker was the young male I had noticed watching me in the parking lot.

"Also, when I had twisted around, I saw that he had a small knife in his hand." Shilling, who had taken self-defense courses, fought desperately for her life. "I went berserk. I began screaming, 'No, no.' I could hear him trying to shush me and that infuriated me. We struggled on the ground and somehow I got my hand into his mouth and dug my fingernails into the soft part under the tongue. I must have hurt him because he bit down on my fingers and then let go of me."

As Guandique ran away, Shilling came across two joggers, who brought her to a police station.

Five weeks later, Guandique would strike in the park again. This time his victim was twenty-six-year-old attorney Christy Wiegand.

"On Sunday, July 1, 2001, I went for a run in Rock Creek Park with my fiance and I will never forget what happened that day," Wiegand recounted in an official police statement. "Being attacked from behind by a man with a knife is the most terrifying thing that has ever happened to me. When my attacker dragged me into the ravine, holding a knife against my throat and covering my mouth, I thought and still think today that he was going to rape me or try to kill me.

"I feared for my life. What struck me most was that within ten seconds, I was off the jogging path in the woods, struggling to scream and out of sight of any passerby. Until that day, I never realized how quickly someone with the advantage and a weapon can put a person in a position of total isolation and helplessness."

When she continued to scream, the attacker fled. Finding her fiance, who had been jogging far ahead of her, Wiegand reported the incident to U.S. Park Police. They captured Guandique on a street near the edge of the park. He was trying to steal the jogger's Walkman to pay his rent, he told police.

In September 2001, Guandique pleaded guilty to the 'acks on the two joggers. In February 2002, he got ten years for each attack and also received a nine-year sentence for breaking into Tomasa's apartment. The jail terms were to be served concurrently, but they ensured that Guandique would spend the next ten years behind bars in a federal prison, since the attacks on the joggers occurred in a national park.

After Chandra's body was found, Gary Condit's attorney, Mark Geragos, was quick to point an accusatory finger at Guandique. After all, the intern had been wearing a jogging bra and exercise shoes and had been carrying a Walkman. Moreover, her body had been found not too far from where Guandique attacked his two victims.

Geragos couldn't have known it at the time, but Guandique had already come under suspicion in the investigation of Chandra's death.

As he sat in jail during the last months of 2001, awaiting sentencing, another inmate contacted cops, telling them Guandique confessed he'd been hired to kill Chandra. But when investigators went to North Carolina to interview Guandique, he denied the account — and passed a lie detector test. The inmate who informed the cops about Guandique failed his own polygraph.

Most significantly, Guandique's modus operandi ultimately did not fit with the crime scene that indicated Chandra had known her attacker.

After Congressman Condit implied in a letter to constituents that Chandra might be the victim of a serial killer, the police also revisited several unsolved murder cases. Two years before Chandra's disappearance, Joyce Chiang, a lawyer for the Immigration and Naturalization Service, disappeared. Her decomposed body was later found in the Potomac River. Five months before Chiang disappeared, Washington intern Christine Mirzayan was raped and murdered while walking home from a barbecue. Chandra, Joyce and Christine all lived in the same area, had dark hair and were in their twenties.

John Walsh, whose TV show *America's Most Wanted* has helped solve hundreds of crimes, said he strongly believed that Chandra was the victim of a sexual predator operating in the nation's capital.

Anything was possible in the unsolved case, but Detectives Durant and Kennedy were coming to certain conclusions on the basis of items that were not found near Chandra's body or in her apartment at the Newport. Her pinky ring set with diamond chips and inscribed with her initials, a gift from her parents, was missing. So was the gold serpentine bracelet Condit had given her. The keys she must have taken with her were also never recovered. And strangely, the police had found nothing in her apartment that indicated she knew the congressman.

Did Chandra's killer remove from her person items that would quickly identify her, like the ring and the bracelet? Suddenly the discovery of Condit throwing the Tag Heuer watch box in a trash can in a park on the outskirts of town takes on added meaning.

Did the killer also clean her apartment of anything linking her to the congressman? That would explain why her keys were missing.

The investigators learned that it was easy to enter the Newport unnoticed, despite the presence of security cameras. No one has a key for the front entrance; even tenants must be buzzed in by security personnel. However, the keys Chandra had carried would have granted access through a rear-alley gate and then a back door into the building where the elevator is just a few feet away.

"You can come in that way, and unless the guard is actually staring at the video screen monitoring that entrance, you'll go unnoticed," said a resident.

"Detectives are wondering if the killer may even have packed Chandra's bags to throw confusion into the search for her," said a law enforcement source. "She wasn't scheduled to leave Washington for a week but the packed bags gave the impression she was leaving immediately."

CHAPTER 28

At the entrance to the auditorium in Modesto Centre Plaza sat giant silver tureens filled with Reese's peanut butter cups, Chandra's favorite candy. The front of the room was lined with bouquets of red and white roses and white gladioli. Blown-up photographs portraying Chandra's life from infant to child to young adult had been placed on easels. In all the pictures, she was smiling.

It was May 28th, and nearly twelve hundred people came to attend the memorial service for the twenty-four-year-old woman whose life ended so brutally. Her skeletal remains were still back in D.C., where just a few hours earlier Medical Examiner Jonathan Arden had officially ruled Chandra's death a homicide.

All along Bob and Susan Levy had held out hope that their daughter was alive somewhere.

"But their worst fears had come true," said Chandra's cousin, Michael Maistelman, a Milwaukee attorney who flew in for the service.

"Devastated" is how he described them.

To reach the auditorium, mourners crossed a red brick bridge over a waterway in the Centre Plaza and funneled through a swarm of news reporters and television commentators dabbing on makeup between live shots.

Chandra's aunt and confidante, Linda Zamsky, had arrived from Maryland days earlier to help out. As the Levys arranged the memorial service, she kept the plants watered, made sure the refrigerator was full, and fed the family's two dogs.

Linda had tried to be the strong one in the thirteen months since her beloved niece disappeared. She had gone public with details of Chandra's affair with Gary Condit. She'd gone on television to keep the case in the spotlight. Now she had no more words, only feelings of pain and heartache, and tears flowed freely.

"I'm too upset to speak," she managed to convey to the press. "I can't make words to describe my feelings. It hit me really hard today."

Many of the mourners were residents of Modesto, there to show the Levys and their relatives that the community shared their sorrow.

"Chandra disappeared over a year ago," said Modesto Mayor Carmen Sabatino. "The city's gone through the Levys' grief, their hope, their realization, and today, their mourning."

Olivia Jara, a home health care worker who lived in town, took the day off to attend the service because, "We feel like she's part of our family, our city."

Alma Goldener came simply because she is a parent, adding, "We just wanted to pay our respects."

Parents of other children who died too young were there to share the Levys' grief. Kathy Wetherbee lost her two-year-old son to a viral infection but expressed that she could only imagine the anguish that Bob and Susan Levy endured for over a year, an anguish intensified with the discovery of her body and confirmation of a murder.

"To go through a year of it is really heartrending," she said. "Such an ordeal they've been through."

Jennifer Baker, the college chum who had explored the wonders of Washington with her good friend, showed up hand-in-hand with Lisa Bracken, one of Chandra's closest friends since high school days. In the months after Chandra disappeared, Baker and Bracken, who had never met, became good friends themselves, a friendship forged by the volunteer work they did during the hunt for the missing intern.

"I saw Jennifer on TV when this happened. I decided I would help out, too," said Bracken, a children's activity director at the Modesto Fitness and Racquet Club. "It's such a stressful thing. It goes through your mind so much. There isn't a day that goes by that I don't think about her."

Kristina Holland, a former resident of nearby Ceres and an independent filmmaker in Los Angeles, was drawn to the service for a different reason. She had been working on a documentary about Condit, following him for several months until the congressman lost the March 5th primary election.

"I've been so absorbed in that," said Holland. "I needed to see the other side. You feel like you know her."

Members of the Modesto Symphony Orchestra String Quartet played in the auditorium foyer, trying to soothe the feelings of loss that hung over the ceremony. Family friend and harpist Donelle Page then contributed traditional Hebrew songs, the Christian hymn *Amazing Grace*, and a favorite of Chandra's, Paul Simon's *El Condor Pasa*.

Susan Levy held a small Beanie Bear as she walked

slowly to a front row in the auditorium with Bob and Adam. For most of the hour-and-a-half service she maintained her composure, as did Bob, although there were moments when the tears could not be controlled.

Adam's touching tribute to his older sister was one of those moments.

"I feel Chandra's presence every day," the twenty-year-old confided to the gathering. "She has never left us. She has just transformed herself into a different form of energy."

It was an energy, he explained, that he actually felt.

"For example, Chandra used to play the piano quite well when she was younger. When she disappeared last summer, I started being able to play. I'd never taken lessons or had any interest in playing the piano. I don't feel this is a coincidence. It's a sign from her that she has transformed part of her being into me and everyone she cared about.

"We were a typical big sister and little brother. Sometimes we fought, sometimes we laughed, and sometimes we drove each other nuts. However, we always loved and cared for each other.

"Although her physical body may be gone, her spirit and memories will live on in all of us. She will never be lost, because she will always remain in our hearts and minds.

"I would like to thank everybody in here for all the support and love for Chandra and our family."

As a memento of the occasion, the Levys printed up copies of a poem that a well-wisher had sent them in the months before Chandra's body was found.

We pray every day that she is returned to you.
Where is Chandra? Only God is to know,
But as time goes on, our fears only grow.

The picture of her is etched in our mind,
The beautiful young lady — a twinkle in her eye,
Such a lovely young lady, who makes her family proud.
Who now express their grief in voices oh so loud.
Please find our daughter, and send her back home.
This house is just a house, it is no longer a home.
She is part of our family, and as all parents know,
Each day your child is missing, fears continue to grow.
Our door remains open, waiting her safe return.
Our love for our daughter forever will burn.
Our faith is in the Lord, who gets us through each day.
From sunrise to sunset, as a family together we pray.
Where is Chandra? Only God is to know.
But as time goes on, our fears only grow.

Five rows behind the Levys sat Anne Marie Smith, the
flight attendant whose own life had been turned upside-
down by Congressman Gary Condit. She was not there for
publicity, a charge the Condit camp had leveled at her
when she came forward in the months after Chandra's disappearance. She was there only to mourn someone she felt
a bond with.

In fact, Anne Marie slipped in and out of the service
unnoticed by most of the press and mourners. The Levys
didn't even know she attended until it was mentioned to
them days after the ceremony.

Also sitting anonymously among the mourners was
Dennis Cardozo, who had unseated Gary Condit in the
March 5th Democratic primary election and would be run-
ning for Congress in the upcoming November election.

As for the disgraced politician, Condit had left it up to his
lawyer, Mark Geragos, to issue a statement about the discovery of Chandra's body. The statement was two sen-

tences long: "Congressman Gary Condit and his family want to express their heartfelt sorrow and condolences to the Levy family. The Levy family will remain in our prayers."

Geragos said he was anticipating that the Levy family would again "lash out" at Condit now that their daughter's body had been found and her death was officially ruled a homicide. He had wisely advised the congressman "to just sit and take it." Condit's mouth was his own worst enemy.

Instead, the Levys chose to dedicate that day only to Chandra. After the memorial service, her godmother, Frannie Iseman, spoke briefly to reporters.

"She brought a lot of joy to us. Although she's not here physically, she's right here," explained Frannie, touching her heart. "And that will never go away." Reminding the press that the name Chandra means "daughter higher than the moon and stars" in Sanskrit, Frannie said when remembering her, the family would look not at the ground but at "the stars."

EPILOGUE

As this book went to print, a federal grand jury investigating the Chandra Levy case continued to call witnesses.

Gary Condit's chief of staff Mike Lynch, who initially denied Condit and Chandra were romantically involved, and Randy Groves, Condit's former legislative aide and press secretary, were called to testify.

Mike Dayton, Condit's top administrative assistant — who was his driver on the suspicious trip to toss out a watch box that had contained a former lover's gift — was also expected to be called, as were friends and acquaintances of the murdered intern.

Testing of Chandra's clothing and her other possessions found near her remains yielded no clues to her killer's identity. Meanwhile, Washington, D.C., Police Chief Charles Ramsey has said detectives will be going back to reinterrogate anyone who may shed light on the murder.

The list, Ramsey pointed out, included Congressman Gary Condit.

****

In September 2002, *Esquire* magazine published an interview with Condit conducted by a reporter named Mike Sager. Allowing Sager to chronicle his last unsuccessful attempt at reelection, including its losing outcome, was a good decision by the former congressman. The article reiterates Condit's long-term record of political achievements, his good looks, and even his "beautiful shade of blue" eyes.

Sager added, "He has a healthy appreciation for a nice ass walking down the street in a pair of jeans."

"I've been portrayed by the press the way they wanted to portray me," Condit argued, pointing a finger at a press corps bent on his demise. He claims the assertions that he had something to do with Chandra Levy's murder are based on nothing but "lies and innuendo ... I don't think anything anybody could ever do can redeem my name. The damage has been done ... What more can I say?"

Condit still refuses to publicly acknowledge his affair with Chandra Levy.

"They want me to say that I did her," Condit admitted to Sager, who described the politician's face as "rearranging itself into a comic mask."

"Not gonna do it!" said Condit, his voice rising. "Not gonna do it!"

TIMELINE

September 2000 — Chandra Levy lands a job as an intern with the U.S. Bureau of Prisons in Washington, D.C. She moves from California to the nation's capital.

October 2000 — Chandra and her friend, Jennifer Baker, visit the office of Levy's congressman, Gary Condit. They all pose for a picture together.

November 2000 — Chandra has begun an affair with Condit.

January 2001 — Chandra asks her Washington, D.C., landlord about breaking her lease to move in with an unidentified boyfriend.

April 7, 2001 — During a family get-together over Passover, Chandra tells her aunt that she expects to marry Condit and have his baby one day.

April 23, 2001 — Chandra's internship at the Bureau of Prisons comes to an end.

April 24, 2001 — Condit claims to have seen Chandra for the last time at his D.C. condo.

April 29, 2001 — Chandra speaks by phone with Condit for the last time. She later leaves a message on her Aunt Linda's answering machine saying, "I have some really big news."

April 30, 2001 — Chandra cancels her membership at the Washington Sports Club in the evening — it is the last time anyone remembers seeing her alive.

May 1, 2001 — Chandra surfs the Internet for several hours compulsively reading any mention of Condit. She leaves her apartment in the afternoon, taking only her keys and a Walkman with her.

May 5, 2001 — Bob Levy, Chandra's father, calls the D.C. police to ask them to check his daughter's apartment.

May 6, 2001 — The Levys call Condit to ask his help in finding Chandra.

May 7, 2001 — Looking at Chandra's phone records, Susan Levy unknowingly stumbles onto the secret pager number her daughter and Condit used during their affair. The congressman returns Susan's call placed to the number, and when asked if he is having an affair with Chandra, denies any romantic involvement with the young woman.

May 10, 2001 — Levy's disappearance becomes public. Condit calls her "a great person and a good friend."

July 6, 2001 — In his third interview with police, Condit finally admits he had an affair with Chandra.

July 10, 2001 — Police search Condit's apartment. Hours earlier he'd been seen disposing of a watch box that had contained a gift from a former lover.

July 13, 2001 — Condit's lawyer, Abbe Lowell, announces that Condit has successfully passed a privately administered lie detector test.

August 23, 2001 — Connie Chung interviews Condit on national TV. He refuses to acknowledge that he had an affair with Chandra.

November 15, 2001 — Condit is subpoenaed by a federal grand jury probing Chandra's disappearance. The jury seeks documents from the congressman.

March 5, 2002 — Condit loses the California Democratic primary and becomes a lame-duck congressman. Soon afterward he is subpoenaed to appear before the grand jury.

April 12, 2001 — Condit testifies before the grand jury. His appearance lasts less than an hour.

May 1, 2002 — Bob and Susan Levy join a vigil outside Chandra's Washington apartment to mark the first anniversary of her disappearance.

May 22, 2002 — Chandra's remains are found in Rock Creek Park.

May 28, 2002 — Chandra's death is officially ruled a homicide, and she is eulogized at a hometown memorial service.

AUTHORS' NOTE

In more than a combined half-century of reporting, we have covered a wide range of captivating, compelling, and in many cases tragic stories — but none more intriguing than the disappearance and death of Chandra Levy. Most of the material in this book is taken from interviews with relevant individuals, transcripts from recorded material, news items and other information uncovered by the investigative team of American Media, Inc. Certain scenes, inner thoughts and dialogue have been dramatically recreated in order to effectively portray the events depicted in this book.

For their help with this book, we gratefully thank: Tony Ballester, Neil Blincow, Bennet Bolton, Debbie Bottcher, Alan Butterfield, Courtney Callahan, Nanette Dubiel, Cliff Dunn, Ray Fairall, Reginald Fitz, Michael Glynn, Richard Gooding, Michael Hanrahan, James Meyers, Bob Michals, Carla Million, Charlie Montgomery, Lycia Naff, Gunnar Penttinen, Alan Smith, John South, and Daryl Wrobel.

Two days after the tearful memorial service for Chandra Levy, the staff of *The National Enquirer* received a note from the Levy family. It read:

> *Thank you for the flowers & support towards helping to find our daughter. We want you to know we appreciate your compassion in finding what really happened.*
>
> *Sincerely, Sue, Bob, & Adam Levy*

We at *The National Enquirer* want to express, most of all, our heartfelt condolences and thanks to the entire Levy family, who have demonstrated such bravery and poise in the face of this terrible tragedy.